BIGGER THAN BRAVERY

BIGGER
THAN
BRAVERY

BLACK RESILIENCE
AND RECLAMATION
IN A TIME OF PANDEMIC

edited by
Valerie Boyd

lookout

LOOKOUT BOOKS
University of North Carolina Wilmington

First printing, November 2022
ISBN: 9781940596471

Cover design by Emily Louise Smith, Amanda Ake, Lauran Jones, Olivia Loorz, and Gabi Stephens for The Publishing Laboratory
Cover illustration © Reyna Noriega

Library of Congress Control Number: 2022938494

Lookout gratefully acknowledges support from the Literary Arts Emergency Fund, administered by the Community of Literary Magazines and Presses, with funding provided by the Mellon Foundation.

The views expressed in this book do not necessarily reflect those of its publishers or sponsors.

LOOKOUT BOOKS
Department of Creative Writing
University of North Carolina Wilmington
601 S. College Road
Wilmington, NC 28403
lookout.org

Valerie Boyd
December 11, 1963–February 12, 2022

The water is one thing, and one thing for miles.
The water is one thing, making this bridge
Built over the water another. Walk it
Early, walk it back when the day grows dim, everyone
Rising just to find a way toward rest again.
We work, start on one side of the day
Like a planet's only sun, our eyes straight
Until the flame sinks. The flame sinks. Thank God
I'm different. I've figured and counted. I'm not crossing
To cross back. I'm set
On something vast. It reaches
Long as the sea. I'm more than a conqueror, bigger
Than bravery. I don't march. I'm the one who leaps.

—Jericho Brown, "Crossing"

Contents

Introduction:
Profit and Loss

Valerie Boyd

My daddy was not a numbers runner—though he was once mistaken for one and arrested.

Back in the 1960s and '70s, playing the numbers was a common pastime in Black neighborhoods in urban communities like Harlem, Chicago, and Atlanta, where I grew up on the west side, somewhere between Bankhead and Collier Heights.

Working men, homemakers, single mothers, and corner dwellers would whisper a three-digit prayer to the neighborhood numbers runner, who'd jot down the wish-fulfilling formula on a betting slip. Years later, state lotteries would offer a similar game, effectively shuttering the businesses of Black numbers runners and bankers. But back in the day, it was a racket controlled by Black men and women in their own communities. Though illegal and sometimes dangerous, it offered the promise of a shaky stepping-stone to better financial days for runners and players alike.

When I was around eight years old, police raided my dad's Texaco franchise and found a coffee-stained desk littered with small slips of paper, each inscribed with mysterious hieroglyphs in my father's lean, jaunty handwriting. The thin sheets, carefully separated from the perforated seams of a miniature writing tablet—not the raggedy chaos of a spiral-bound notebook—were profit and loss statements for the day, the week, the month. The stacked papers fit neatly into the breast pocket of his light-blue work shirt, stitched with his name, *Roger*, in loose, cursive letters. My mom jokingly referred to that pocket as his "office," and it was filled, seam to seam, with the scrawls of three-digit codes, just as baffling as the ones police found on the underutilized desk—and apparently just as incriminating.

When he rang my mom from a pay phone at the Fulton County Jail, we three kids were incredulous, and our mom was indignant. Roger Boyd was an upstanding citizen, a respected businessman, a deacon in the Baptist Church, a young pillar of the community who comported himself with the understated Alabama dignity of Hank Aaron. On Sundays, when he wasn't in his blue work uniform, he wore dark gray, blue, and black suits like John Lewis, Andrew Young, and the other civil rights titans he admired, though they were his peers, age-wise, and occasionally dropped by his Texaco for gas and a complimentary window wash. Full service.

When my dad finally came home, late into the night, he regaled us with stories of his day in jail, and he laughed at the case of mistaken identity. I don't recall him being enraged or insulted or frightened. Maybe he felt all of those things, but if he did, he didn't say.

During the height of the oil crisis in the mid-1970s, when the nation faced crippling petroleum shortages and steeply elevated gas prices, my dad couldn't afford the gas to keep his Texaco stocked. One day, he rushed home and announced in a tumble of words: "All the money in the house; I need it right now!" At ten years old, I had managed to save about fifty hard-earned dollars. A part of me thought my money was a secret and maybe I could get away with not offering it up to the family cause. But I knew we were bound to starve or thrive together. I turned over my piggy bank, and the gas station survived another week.

Soon after, though, my dad gave up the Texaco—one of the few such Black-owned franchises in the South—and spent a week at home in his undershirt and socks looking at newspaper want ads.

For as long as I could remember, he had been up and at 'em by seven, having his second cup of coffee with my mom, then onto his day as the Great Provider. I had never seen my dad work for The Man—hell, *he* was The Man—and I'd certainly never seen him sit on the couch during the workday with no shoes on.

As I watched him flip through the classifieds of the *Atlanta Constitution*, I briefly wondered if our family life as I knew it was over. In his thirties then, he had a wife who was a stay-at-home mom and three children to support. I imagine he must have felt immense pressure, but—to us, at least—he didn't say.

The next thing I knew, he'd rented a small building on Bankhead Highway, a couple of miles away from his old gas station. Someone hand-painted the sign for him: BOYD'S TIRE & WRECKER SERVICE. He still had the tow truck from the gas station. As long as people were driving cars, they'd need tires, he reasoned, and this would be his great comeback. It was a moment of glory for us all; my mom, my two brothers, and I believed in him and banded together in our family business.

On Sundays after church, we opened the shop for afternoon sales. The building, which my mom persistently called

"The Milk Jug" in honor of its past life as a drive-through convenience store, was so small that the tires and the humans couldn't all fit at once. She and I worked the cash register inside while my dad worked the customers outside—my brothers watching him and memorizing. It was like an alternative happy ending to *A Raisin in the Sun*. Dad eventually moved the business to a larger building down the street, where he remained for thirty-five years before reluctantly retiring.

When Dad passed away on Wednesday, July 8, 2020, we weren't ready.

We had just bought him a new mattress and box springs for Father's Day, so he could get a more comfortable night's rest—not knowing we'd be ushering him to his final resting place so soon. My college-age niece, grounded at home by the pandemic, was assembling the box springs inside the small brick house that my dad shared with my older brother, Mike. Father and son stepped outside to give her more space. When my dad leaned against his walker, it rolled away, and he fell.

A broken hip is a tough diagnosis at age eighty-two. Covid-19 prevented us from visiting him in the hospital, but his surgery went well. It looked like he'd spend a few weeks in rehab, then come home. We were relieved, until Mike began to receive disoriented calls from Dad in the middle of the night. "Why haven't y'all come to visit me?" he demanded, seeming to forget everything he knew about the pandemic. "Come get me out of here!"

My brother would remind him that hospital rules didn't allow us to visit, but that we'd been speaking to him and his caregivers every day.

During the waking hours, he seemed lucid again when we talked with him. On what turned out to be his final full day on earth, he called each of his three children individually. His voice was as relaxed as it had been nearly fifty years earlier, when he'd told us of his escapades in jail that day he was mistaken for a numbers runner. When I asked what he needed, he said, "Nothing. I'm just calling to check on you, to make sure you're all right." The Great Provider. The Protector. The Dependable Dad. If he was worried about getting well, or how much time he had left, he didn't say.

The next day, a nurse called. He had developed pneumonia and was having trouble breathing. They were moving him to the ICU, and we should get there as soon as possible. Before we could find our keys, he was gone.

Mike—who'd worked since he was fourteen alongside the man he called Pop—had been our father's housemate for the past several years. "I don't have any friends anymore," Mike said through tears. "He was my confidante; he was my best friend."

My younger brother, Tim, and I took stoic, silent solace in the fact that his exit was swift and he didn't suffer long. My niece, Mike's daughter, Kaylisha, said the loss of her grandpa messed her up, but she still made us laugh. "At least he's reunited with his boo-thang," she said, referring to my mom, Laura Jean Boyd, who'd passed on in 2013, on Good Friday. They'd been married for fifty-five years.

We weren't ready. We still aren't. When Dad died, he "left us to act out our ceremonies over unimportant things," as the great Zora Neale Hurston wrote of her own mother's death. And so we acted out our ceremonies—muted though they were. Instead of the three-hundred-person homegoing celebration that a man of my father's stature should have had, the pandemic forced us to speed through a ten-minute, masked graveside funeral with fewer than ten attendees. Just his three kids, his one grandchild, and a few close cousins and friends.

People I don't even know still call my brother, outraged

that we buried Roger Boyd—businessman and pillar of the community—and didn't let them know, that we didn't give them a chance to say their own good-byes to a truly good man.

We regret their disappointment, but we have had to reckon with a harsh reality of the pandemic: maybe every Black funeral can't be an hours-long affair, punctuated by a respectful recitation of the deceased's favorite scripture, a sober intoning of his favorite hymn, and a gut-wrenching rendition of "Precious Lord, Take My Hand."

Maybe a swift, stand-up funeral now has its place in the pantheon of Black grief rituals. After all, as Toni Morrison wrote in her slender 1973 masterpiece, *Sula*, we must meet some feelings on our feet. "Then they left their pews. For with some emotions one has to stand."

Queen Mother Morrison elaborated: "They spoke, for they were full and needed to say. They swayed, for the rivulets of grief or of ecstasy must be rocked. And when they thought of all that life and death locked into that little closed coffin they danced and screamed, not to protest God's will but to acknowledge it and confirm once more their conviction that the only way to avoid the Hand of God is to get in it."

We finished the ceremony, gave and received masked hugs, and were back in our cars in less than twelve minutes. The quick, efficient funeral reminded me of my dad's profit and loss statements, packed neatly in his shirt-pocket office.

As we mourned the colossal loss of Roger Boyd, it was the hardest of hard days. But when the sun came out and drenched our little family of strivers in kaleidoscopic light, I considered that magical sunlight a gain. I knew my father—somehow, somewhere—was to thank for it.

In this anthology, thirty-one Black writers take stock of what we've gained and what we've lost, of what the pandemic has taken from us and what it's taught us. Together—in poetry and prose that is both public and private, intimate and expansive—these literary artists model and embody resistance, resilience, and hope.

Karen Good Marable, Deesha Philyaw, and Imani e Wilson, for example, each offer their own singular takes on the music that has carried us through these trying times. When reports of surging Covid-19 rates and rising racist encounters collide on the news, Karen whisks her pre-K daughter off on neighborhood joyrides, imploring Aminé to help her take her baby girl from invisible to "Invincible" in a single bound. Meanwhile, Imani leans on the music of the Black Church to remind herself that "Through It All," she is "blessed and highly favored," as we say. At the same time, Deesha makes a playlist to chronicle the stages of her pandemic life and the tracks of her tears.

Daniel B. Coleman, Aunjanue Ellis-Taylor, Josina Guess, and Jasmin Pittman Morrell contemplate their own mortality as they each personally wrestle the strange beast called Covid. Through a lingering coronavirus haze, Aunjanue turns on the television and watches the insurrection of January 6, 2021, unfold in real time. Sobering questions rush through her mind: "What will happen when the cameras leave? Who will restore the House to order? Who will clean the blood off the floors? Who will pick up the trash left…by these looters?" No doubt, Black women who clean will be expected to do much of this work, she laments in her essay.

Many months later, Josina fights a post-vaccine breakthrough infection. In the middle of summer 2021, she holds whole cloves in her mouth until she can taste their Christmas spice. She tells herself she is getting better, if only she can surrender to healing.

A stunning lineup of poets—from Honorée Fanonne Jeffers

to Alice Walker—distill their fantasies and fears (*ours* too) into the leanest of words, ripe with the lushest of emotions.

Meanwhile, Destiny O. Birdsong, Jason Reynolds, and Shay Youngblood all write about the sustaining power of food—our family recipes, our fearless creativity in the kitchen—and the deeper ways we find to feed our souls.

Days before a knee became George Floyd's noose, Jason buys a barbecue grill and sets out to follow in his father's footsteps as an expert in the art of char. "Food was getting me through the carousel days and circus weeks. It was anchoring me to myself," he writes. "Food made me…full. In all the ways."

Consider *Bigger Than Bravery* an offering, a modest sacrament to help us fill the empty places within. A thoughtful convergence of poetry and essays, the book is organized so that the pieces are in intimate conversation with one another, with the poems serving as deep breaths between the longer narrative essays. If you allow, this book can be a long exhalation, a silent prayer, a solace and a comfort as we reach toward the promise of brighter days ahead.

Black folks of my dad's generation have a famous saying, a defiant flex against any attempts to limit their personal freedom. If I said to my dad, for instance, "Dad, you *have* to stop trying to go to church during the pandemic. You *have* to stay home," he would defend his weekly visits to Greater New Light Missionary Baptist, a church he cofounded, by propping himself up against that old saying: "I don't *have* to do nothing—except pay taxes, stay Black, and die." Those were the absolutes, the nonnegotiables, the only things Black folks of his generation felt they *had* to do.

Here, at the end, my father and this moment in history have taught me that even those absolutes aren't absolute—that we can be free of those requirements too.

Back in the 1990s, when my dad was in his fifties, I was shocked to learn that he had gotten behind in paying his taxes. As the family business grew, his shirt-pocket profit and loss statements became overwhelming, and he let things go for a minute. I convinced him to hire a friend of mine, an excellent young accountant, and she helped him get back on track.

Now I'm in my fifties. A tough medical diagnosis a couple of years ago, followed by the onset of the pandemic, knocked me off my feet for a minute too, and—being my father's daughter—I had to set something down, to let something go. I found myself falling behind in filing my taxes. I'm now working with that same friend—still an amazing, compassionate accountant—on getting back on track, and my father's example, as always, continues to serve me well.

Staying Black—as Imani Perry points out in her essay in this book—is a joy, not a burden. But the pandemic has altered that calculus, too. For decades, I admit, I have taken my Blackness for granted. I assumed that when my father left this earthly plane, we'd have a big Black traditional funeral, a large repast featuring potato salad from multiple competing cooks. Instead, I spent the weekend after the stand-up funeral trying in vain to re-create my mother's peerless recipe.

Even as the pandemic warned us of the fleeting nature of life itself, I took for granted that, in staying Black, I would one day soon attend a literary reading, somewhere in Black America, where I'd slyly catch the smiling eyes, rising just above her mask, of the poet Kamilah Aisha Moon. I took for granted the distinctly Black and beautiful probability that I'd be able to thank her in person for the breathtaking poems she contributed to this volume. But, like my father, she has quietly exited the earthly stage and is no longer here for a sister's embrace.

Staying Black no longer feels like something I can take

for granted. The essays and poems in this book remind and inspire me to cultivate my Blackness with thoughtfully curated activities. Like frequent jaunts to Savannah to enjoy the cuisine that master chef Mashama Bailey serves at The Grey, her exquisite restaurant in a formerly segregated Georgia bus station. Like finding my way to Sunday service at the Full Gospel Tabernacle Church in Memphis, founded in 1976 by the Reverend Al Green, who still preaches at the modest Tennessee church almost weekly.

And then there's the dying part—the biggest myth of all.

Death, my dad has taught me, is a ruse. A life well-lived is its own reward, and once the transcending spirit lays the worn and weary body down, there is rest and restoration. My father is now an influential ancestor, I believe, having achieved a kind of omniscience that empowers him to work subtly on my behalf in the spirit world and on this mortal plane.

My father's ancestral presence lifts me up as I join hands with the other writers in this book to offer you, dear reader, a glimpse into your own bravery, your own greatness, your own transcendent freedom.

My dad's good friend, the Reverend James L. Green, the founding pastor at Greater New Light, used to end every worship service with a paraphrase of Luke 14:22. As we offer you this book—this secular and sacred bible of profit and loss, this chronicle of all that we have endured and enjoyed, all that we've lost and found—Rev. Green's words feel like the right way to end, and to begin again: "We have done as the Lord has commanded, yet there is room."

BIGGER THAN BRAVERY

Char

Jason Reynolds

May of 2020 I bought a barbecue grill. My first. I grew up with one of those men who considered himself a grill master, excited about letting the coal burn off, and serious about basting and watching, turning and poking. Burgers and ribs and chicken and shrimp and, quite frankly, anything else fit for flame. If it was edible, according to my father, it could be made more delectable through the ancient and mysterious craft of grilling. His belief was that it is a deceptively simple practice, and that the complicated keys to it all are temperature and timing. If the grill is too hot, the meat will be raw inside. If left on too long, the meat will burn. The perfect char comes from harnessing the heat for the right amount of time, and if you're skilled enough to do it right, the fire should elevate the natural flavors of the flesh. Though his ideas around grilling were philosophical, he used the act of it as a substitute for campfire. A place to hover and connect over story. A place to thaw.

Now here I was, thirty-seven years old and finally eager to learn. I hadn't been outside in months. Covid-19 had become the sky and ground, and we were indefinitely locked away in quarantine, settling into the fact that our lives as we'd known them would be forever altered. For me, this experience felt less out-of-body, and more *into-body*. Like I'd been forced into a dark well of self, tumbling down a bottomless shaft. Etched into its walls were images of all I'd been ignoring and avoiding through years of relentless work and travel. I also hadn't seen my father in months. Not since he had been given a prognosis that the cancer was still there. A pulsing remnant, small but determined, hiding in a nook of his body no surgeon could successfully get to.

Looking back now, I realize I bought this hunk of metal for these reasons: to give myself permission to discover a new part of myself while also discovering what I hoped would be some extra connection between me and my old man. Something else I could say was ours. I mean, he'd given me so much already: my complexion, a beard, a barrel chest, a baritone voice, a sense of humor, a constitution, an ego. He'd given me most of what I'd known about my own inner-workings, and yet, everything I knew had been upended by illness, his and the world's, simultaneously compounding.

A few days later, George Floyd was killed by a police officer in Minneapolis. I could state the officer's name here, but I see no need to name every organic element that makes up a disease. Floyd's death was a moment during which the world watched, over and over, a knee become a noose. I don't pretend to understand why white people decided to care when they decided to care, but I know how ugly it feels to wish I, a Black man, could turn it off. To wish I could just swallow the stone, or quell the belly-churning. I watched, wept for a man my older brother's age, then tried to dislocate my feelings. I tried to find a place to put them, but most of my corners were already occupied by other ornate trunks of painful ephemera.

I'd do this again when the protests started. Stand in the window watching my neighbors, friends, teenagers—everyone out of work and school—take to the street, wailing the names of George Floyd and Breonna Taylor, pushing their voices through bandannas and medical masks, no fabric thick enough to muffle the fed-up. I watched it on television. I watched it on my phone. I watched it, and watched it, feeling small and embarrassed because I could not join. Soon I'd have an opportunity to see my father, and I needed to make sure I was healthy enough to sit with him. It's strange to want people to know you're with them when you're not with them. Strange for absence to bring about such shame, though I could never actually be absent from this. But there was something killing my dad, also. Something unfair and unwarranted. He, too, was reaching out in need.

He called me that afternoon, my father. He called often, but on that day he wanted to talk about what happened to George Floyd. He needed to express his anger and tell me about how painful it was to see. I couldn't imagine what it must've been like to watch from his hospital bed. To have to feel his ailing body ache for George and have to clear the water from his eyes whenever a nurse came to check his vitals. I could hear the somber in his shaky voice, his heart clawing at the world on behalf of his own children. Eventually he steadied and spun into other things, sober confessions and apologies for instances long forgiven, but mostly memories of the two of us.

"I was the first person you ever met," he boasted. "Your mother had a C-section, so when they pulled you out, they handed you right to me." He loved telling this story, and told

it often. Loved knowing he was my first friend, my introduc-
tion to the world. While he dawdled down memory lane, I inevitably asked him the things that seemed most prescient.

"Are you scared?"

"Of what, death?"

"Yeah."

Through the phone, I could almost hear his skin tighten
under rising cheekbones. "Son, I've never been afraid to live,
so I've never been afraid to die." Then came the slurping of
water, just something to wet his lips.

After a series of *I love yous* and *call me tomorrows*, we hung
up. I'd hear my father's voice again throughout the rest of the
day, droning on in my head. And I'd see George Floyd's face
again on the afternoon news in-between coronavirus updates,
and on the evening news in-between uprising updates. And on
every timeline.

And I knew he was afraid to die.

And I knew I was afraid to live.

I was afraid to tell my father about the grill I'd just purchased, because soon he would no longer be able to eat; his
ability to swallow, stolen. There was no way I could torture
him by telling him about my culinary plans. Not after years of
him bragging about his venison, or his shrimp kabobs, or even
him tricking me and my older brother into eating squirrel and
rabbit when we were children. Not after pepper challenges
and hours spent cracking open the shells of beer-boiled blue
crabs. Food, especially grilled food, had always been a point of
pride for him, and eating with us over the years seemed to give
him extra vertebrae. But his serving was up. His plate pulled
from the table. His apron, hung. And now it was my turn to
man the fire, to take the tongs, but I couldn't tell him how
excited I was to do so. I just couldn't. Perhaps he would've

dubbed me the new grill master of the family, but there was no way I could risk it.

Food was getting me through the carousel days and circus weeks. It was anchoring me to myself. Imagine some inner form of yourself, small and floating around in your own skin, bumping against your own walls, and the outer form of you is wondering where all the discomfort is coming from. Just like with my father, food made me...full. In all the ways. Not just eating it, but cooking it. Preparing it.

I'd learned to cook at a young age and had been in the kitchen since I was nine. I would take my father's steaks from the freezer—after graduating from Steak-umms—and cook them in my mother's cast-iron pan for my friends. It was my greatest magic trick. My version of the backflip. I knew how to tenderize, how to season, how to know when the meat was done. But as I got older and moved out, times were either feast or famine. If there was famine, I ate sandwiches and Top Ramen. In times of feast, I ate out at a different restaurant every night. Not because I was rich—I wasn't—but because this is what life is like for many young adults living in major cities. There are so many things to taste: cuisines from around the world, local faves. Gathering spots where the stars of a neighborhood constellate for a few hours a night. I lived this way through most of my twenties and all of my thirties.

Until March of 2020.

Until Covid and quarantine.

Until restaurants and cafes shuttered, suddenly leaving me searching, trying to remember who I was at nine years old. Where was my mother's pan, my father's steak, the recipes? So I reintroduced myself to the stove, and after a while my love for cooking returned and metastasized, growing and changing. I purchased a new Dutch oven, a saucepan, invested in mixing bowls and steamer baskets, all sorts of knives and tweezers, spoons and colanders.

And then, after basically overhauling my kitchen, came the next logical piece—the grill.

The first thing I tried was a whole snapper. I scored it, seasoned it, stuffed it with fresh aromatics—garlic, oregano, thyme, rosemary. Then I brushed it with a little oil and laid it on the hot grate. It sizzled as the fire jumped, licking its flesh from below. And as the herbs, activated by the heat, danced in the vapor, I was a little boy again standing with my father, watching his hands brush over the meat. I could smell the beer on his breath in the breeze. I could hear the metal scraping as he closed the lid. I could hear his brothers and his friends, their wisecracks and sermons about white folks and the ways of the world.

After a few minutes, I flipped the fish. Again, I could hear it cooking. I could hear the world cooking, also. My neighbors talking about the protests. People shouting on my street, the cars, honking in solidarity. The sun on my face, as I lifted the lid of the grill, a billow of smoke signaling that I was here— still here—and also there with them. With George Floyd. With Breonna Taylor. With all those struggling to breathe. I was just trying to get my temperature and timing right so that I might find joy, just for a moment, in this charred thing. I was trying to see what my dying father saw in the grill. That it could be a campfire where I could and would tell myself stories. Remind myself of who I am in my devastated family and this broken world. That if I can learn to harness the heat, flame on flesh might awaken something in the meat.

The Quarantine Album: Liner Notes

Deesha Philyaw

These are the songs my mind whispers into the night, screams into the void, and whistles when the sun peeks through the clouds at me.

Track 1: Who's Zoomin' Who

I divide my Zoom calls into two categories: those that require me to wear a bra, and those that do not. One thing about this pandemic: it has stripped me down to the essentials. Is a bra really necessary? Are panties? A car? I drive only once or twice a month now, usually to the post office to mail copies of my book, occasionally to the grocery store for items that my Instacart shopper tells me aren't in stock. Random things I need for all the cooking I'm doing these days: fresh rosemary, lump crabmeat, key lime juice. Instacart, Grubhub, and Zoom, the new holy trinity of my days and nights. Most of the Zoom calls are part and parcel of my book tour. Some are related to the project manager contract gig I have that pays me well and gives me the flexibility to also do a virtual book tour. A few Zoom calls are social: movie watch parties (no bra), happy hours (bra), coworking situations (no bra), celebrations (bra). And one Zoom call was a date (bra).

Track 2: It's the End of the World

I released a book during the pandemic. My debut short-story collection reached the Black women I had hoped it would reach. I'm winning awards. Hollywood came calling. I'm being paid to talk about writing. I have no boss, and I can afford health insurance. All of this while the pandemic rages, surges. In the U.S., over half a million people (and counting) are dead, needlessly so. We saw the end, though not the last, of a white supremacist president enabled by a Congress made up of other white supremacists, liars, crooks, cowards, Maxine Waters, and a handful of other righteous public servants. Our flimsy alleged democracy survived an attempted coup of this deeply compromised, bought-and-sold government. In his last six months in office, the bloodthirsty monster of a president resumed federal executions after a seventeen-year hiatus, killing thirteen people on death row, more than any other president in more than 120 years. Black people continue to be murdered on the street and in their homes; their killers continue to not face any sort of justice. As of this writing, thousands of Black families in Mississippi haven't had clean water for more than three weeks now, the result of decades of systemic racism and indifference, and an unprecedented cold snap precipitated by climate change. Children are still in cages. Politicians are still playing in our faces. We are holding on by threads. There's so much fear and death, Black death, and cruelty, that one day something is going to crack under the weight of all of this, and that something may be me, but right now, this year, I'm having the best time of my professional life. And sometimes, I don't know how to feel. And sometimes, I do what Black folks have always done: let a shout of celebration and wail of sorrow live side by side in my throat. One day, a couple of years ago, a well-known writer gave voice to something I now feel. Shortly after winning a major literary prize, the writer tweeted that he'd won this big prize and still couldn't get a date. I recently tried to find that tweet, but I couldn't. Perhaps the writer deleted the tweet because he worried, as I sometimes do, about appearing "thirsty," as the kids say. God forbid we admit to feeling lonely, even in a pandemic when it's now more acceptable to say that you're lonely. God forbid we feel parched and crave something cool and comforting.

Track 3: Gonna Make You Sweat

I play a game nearly every day called, "Is it Menopause Night Sweats and Hot Flashes, or Covid-19?" A biological fact: People sweat more under stressful conditions. Every day since March 2020 has been a stressful condition, so I'm sweating around the clock and around parts of my body where I don't recall ever sweating before. On Zoom calls, heat from my face causes the bottom of my glasses to fog up. I wonder if anyone notices.

Track 4: Computer Love

I set out to write a song about the shame and stigma attached to feeling lonely for lack of a romantic partner. But because of the shame and stigma attached to feeling lonely for lack of a romantic partner, I almost didn't write this song. A friend posted on Facebook about missing touch, missing sexual intimacy. Immediately, his comments section was flooded by people urging him to love himself, reminding him that he's awesome and enough. We DMed later that evening about how infuriating those comments were, how his lament was not the dreaded "centering of romantic love." We assured each other that it's okay to want to lie in bed like spoons with someone, to miss sex, and to be sad about it. We talked about how the problem isn't just not having the intimacy you want. It's not knowing when you will have it again that's so crushing. We talked about how wanting badly to be kissed on the mouth with tongues doesn't mean you don't appreciate the love of family and friends. Speaking of which, I'm currently in ten group chats across multiple apps with different configurations of family and friends, some more active than others. One of the chats is a little group called Party at the Pandemic. In it, some friends and I rant and clown and swap recipes, laugh at memes, and share articles about touch deprivation. We cheer each other on in our virtual professional events. We created this chat to be the kind of place where you can say outright that you're lonely, but no one ever does. I did mention once that I "met" someone on Match who I thought was promising. I haven't yet told the chat how that situation went south soon after.

Track 5: The Tracks of My Tears

A friend had told me about his teeth cleaning experience, about how the hygienist brushing up against him was the first physical contact he'd had in months, so I thought I was prepared. But when I went in for my cleaning appointment, I found myself tearing up behind the protective goggles as soon as the hygienist fastened the bib around my neck. I didn't make any sound, but I was still embarrassed. I explained to the hygienist that I hadn't been that close to anyone but my children in months. She told me not to worry, that I wasn't the first person who had reacted that way. I don't know if that was true, or if she just said it to make me feel better, but it did make me feel better.

Track 6: If That's Your Boyfriend…

Before the pandemic, my friend Kiese found a book that made him wish for "a book club for lonely grown folks who aren't all the way lonely or all the way grown." That book was *Hard* to *Love*, a collection of essays by Briallen Hopper, in which she looks at love outside of the traditional romantic and familial framing. Newly divorced for the second time, I had dog-eared so many pages in that book. Fast forward to the present moment of isolation: these are the perfect conditions to explore an intimate friendship, or what some people call a platonic romance. I skirt along the edges of this with a friend who lives in another country, and with other friends of all genders in text messages and video calls where we say "I love you," check in with each other, and demonstrate care more deeply and more frequently than before. But the body wants what it wants, and mine wants to be held, and made love to. I want a partner, a steady, a person to wake up next to again and again. "Your book is your boyfriend," says my friend Wednesday, a *New York Times* bestselling author. What she means is, the busyness of promoting my book and reveling in all of the opportunities it affords me will take up most of my time and attention. What she means is, my book will distract me from wanting sex and companionship. I wish this were true. I wish the euphoria from all the good book news was an adequate substitute for sex and companionship.

Track 7: All the Single Ladies
Someone tweets, "Check on your single friends. We are not okay." And we're not. We're touch-starved and weary. But truth be told, some of us weren't okay before the pandemic. Some of us live in a city simultaneously deemed the "most livable" in the country and the worst in the country for Black people, especially Black women, by every socioeconomic measure there is. (Lesson: if something is the worst for Black people, but the best for everyone else, just ignore the unpleasant reality for Black people, and focus on happy things, like our mayor does.) Some of us had already given up hope of

finding a partner in this city. I doubt that I will find one here, not as long as I have standards. Someone I follow tweeted to the Twitterverse, "Why are you so easily impressed? Look for a real show, not an empty theater." And I felt proud that I've learned not to settle for an empty theater, that I'm holding out for a real show.

Track 8: Brandy

In October, a month before the Gaslighter-in-Chief got the boot, one of my pugs died. Caramel was almost eleven and a very good boy. I spent nearly three months' rent hoping to save him. I wanted my kids to know that we did everything we could. I felt helpless. Now, Caramel's sister and littermate, Fudgie, is on my book tour with me. For every event, she is at my feet or in my lap. Her grief and separation anxiety are stark. Sometimes, it even overwhelms me, the way she follows me everywhere. I feel drained by her neediness, by the dozen times each day I cradle her and carry her up a flight of stairs, by her anxious poops whenever I fail to bring her upstairs with me, or take too long to return. I have to remind myself that she's confused. She doesn't know where her brother went. We both miss Caramel. Only, I'm also missing someone else too. But I don't know his name.

Track 9: Stir Fry

When my deadlines approach or are missed, I cook less and order in more. When a writer I follow tweeted, "All I do is order food and cry," I felt so seen.

Track 10: Somebody That I Used to Know

There's no such thing as casual sex or casual dating anymore. Or rather, the definition of *casual* has changed. Because there's nothing casual about an interaction with someone who could wipe out you and your entire family. The need to vet someone and deem them trustworthy is essential. In the Before Time, you might find out a person was lying about being single or what they did for a living. Annoying, but it wouldn't kill you. When I finally break down and have masked sex, four months into the pandemic, it's with someone I've known and trusted for a while. He worried the whole time that I felt used, that the masked sex felt transactional. I tried to assure him that it just felt...sad. I told myself right then that sad sex is not better than no sex at all. Afterward, we sat six feet apart, still naked and masked, and talked about our jobs and our respective daughters. When he texted me again a few weeks later—*hey Superstar*—I didn't respond.

Track 11: It's a Man's World

When writing about being unpartnered and lonely, one risks being thought of as undesirable in a culture where women who aren't desired might as well not exist. But being desired isn't my problem. It's *mutual* desire that has proved elusive. On Instagram, a troll tells Halle Berry that she can't "keep" a man. Halle claps back, "Who said I wanted to keep them?" I feel that. I could have a man, but the pickings are slim. There's the guy who put a Cosby rape joke in his dating app profile. There's the one I went on a date with (pre-pandemic, of course) who excused himself to the restroom and never returned, after getting upset because I referred to our server using the pronoun they. And though it didn't happen to me, I think of a beautiful single friend who tells me that men either fetishize or insult her fat body—well, except for the married man with twins on the way who desperately wanted to make her the center of his second life. We're expected to keep patching ourselves up and bouncing back from so much hurt and disappointment, to be fresh and open and not bitter toward men who offer so little, even when the world isn't falling apart. And when the world is falling apart, none of us are at our best, but some good company sure would be nice.

Track 12: Before I Let Go

This is the song about how the situation with the promising guy from Match—the one I thought was a real show, not an empty theater—went south. His opening act was solid. He was smart, funny, principled, willing to travel, and smitten. I allowed myself to become smitten too. He showed up, virtually, and didn't play games. We were vulnerable with each other, both too old to play coy, or play at anything, really. We often talked late into the night. All cards on the table. Then I felt something shift. And bless him, when I told him, he didn't tell me I was imagining it. When I told him I suspected he had some healing to do, and that I needed to step away and let him heal, he told me he was scared. That I was the most incredible woman he'd ever met, and he didn't deserve me. That I deserved someone already full-grown who could love me right. But that he knew the most loving thing he could do was let me walk away. *I appreciate your honesty, brother. I appreciate that you didn't turn your fear into a weapon and hurt me. I appreciate your not wasting my time. But damn. Damn.*

Haircut, May 2020 in Decatur, GA

Kamilah Aisha Moon

I'm taking a chance
today—I need
to do something
for myself,
something I need
another to do.

In my barber's home
instead of the shop,
her young daughter
watches cartoons
in the living room
like it's normal
that she's not
in school.

Eyes smiling above
our masks
the entire time,
we speak of how
we've been faring,
our fears when
her fingers
lay across my scalp

& begin their nimble work.
Hmmm, the first touch

since hugging my family
in TN good-bye
in March, unsure
of everything,
every thing
but their love.

Just Like Now

Pearl Cleage

As we adjust to living in the time of the virus, people keep wanting me to write about these strange, terrifying days, but it's too soon. It's like trying to write about a tsunami when you're hoping like hell that you're still running ahead of the wave. The thing is, I know why they're asking me. Writing is what I do. It's how I process the world around me and the worlds inside my head, equally complex tasks to which I have devoted my life. Without that process, I am subject to all manner of confusion and mental mayhem. I think that mayhem is what folks are hoping I can help them avoid when they ask me to put some thoughts on paper about this moment. I get it, but I can't do it. This moment is too scary. I'm not ready to write about ventilators and mass graves and terrified people dying alone, separated from their anguished loved ones who are unable to hold their hands and help them cross over. Context is crucial.

I'm too young to remember the 1918 flu pandemic, but I'm old enough to have been present at the start of the AIDS epidemic when we didn't even have a name for it yet. What we had were some whispered warnings about a mysterious cancer that was killing gay men. As a child of the '60s, I was lucky enough to achieve sexual agency at a time when the pill had greatly simplified the challenge of reliable birth control and there were few venereal diseases that could not be cured with antibiotics. Then all of a sudden, there was AIDS. Confined to no one community or sexual practice, despite vain hetero hopes that certain sexual preferences would equal salvation, no one was immune. AIDS turned our fantasy pursuit of no-risk, non-monogamous love affairs into an urgent real-life public health campaign that drew us a picture with this sobering fact: *When you have sex with him, you have sex with all the people he's had sex with.* There was a cartoon of two stick figures holding hands, then their lovers and then their lovers' lovers, and on and on in a colorful stick figure pyramid, encouraging us to consider the consequences of indiscriminate, unprotected sex. And we did.

It was hard to avoid the warnings. I had gay friends who regularly reported the devastation that was already reaching into crowded Midtown Atlanta bars and prowling the Piedmont Park cruising trails with equal ferocity. Concerned for the health of my best friend, who I knew often enjoyed a late-night ramble on those same trails, I asked him if he was using condoms—at that time, the best first line of defense.

"Sometimes," he said, smiling sheepishly. "Sometimes." That's when I knew we were in big trouble. Any cure that depends on human beings exercising their best judgment when there is the promise, or even the possibility, of sex in the air is doomed from the start. So I hugged my friend and he made us a couple of vodka and tonics and we spent the afternoon watching the fat fish in his koi pond and pretending that "sometimes" was in any way a sensible response to my question.

I've been thinking about those times a lot lately. I've been remembering the challenge of getting people to protect themselves from a disease that they hadn't known existed only a few months ago. I remembered that the widespread resistance to common sense public health measures was often rooted in our absolute terror of the unknown. In those days, just like now, that terror sometimes led to a resigned fatalism. "If it's my time, it's just my time, so what's the point of a condom?" Sometimes, just like now, it led to a defiant refusal to take the virus seriously. "I don't look good in a mask." This kind of denial, what my husband, Zeke, calls "belligerent ignorance," manifests itself in people refusing to wear masks or observe even a few feet of social distancing when that's the least we can do to stay safe. It shows up in angry confrontations as stores reopen and customers demand the right to taunt the virus once removed by sneezing on the rest of us who are only dashing in to see if they've finally got any toilet paper. I watched a man on TV screaming about his constitutional right to shop without a mask and then a video of an angry woman whose refusal to wear one or shop elsewhere escalated into a viral video of her arrest.

Sometimes it seems like we haven't learned very much at all in the forty years since the AIDS epidemic changed our lives forever. There is the same denying and the same demonizing and the same sad willingness to speak of an acceptable number of deaths so long as it's not me or people who look like me doing the dying. Watching the American death toll climbing, I remembered those days when we wondered how we could possibly live through the loss of so many friends, so many lovers, so many who were the best of us.

And then I remembered. In the depth of our despair, there was always a moment. A moment when you had to either surrender to that fear and darkness or decide you were going to live as big and bold and bright as you could for as long as you could and then do it. In those moments, I think we remembered our capacity for joy. Even when we're scared or angry or confused or deeply sad, there was, and is, at the center of our being, a belief in the power of love if we take the time to look and then act on what we see.

So that is my challenge. I have to see the joy so I can be the joy. Sometimes it's hard. Especially if I watch too much cable news, but sometimes my friends make it easy. Take last week. My friend Eugene Russell—composer, actor, musician, and family man—pulled up under my magnolia tree, hopped out of his car with his saxophone, stopped at a safe distance, and played "Lean on Me," right in the middle of my front walk. Zeke and I stood on the front porch, swaying and singing because if you can't sing "Lean on Me" in front of your own house in the middle of a pandemic, when can you?

No sooner had replaced his mask and departed, trailing music in the air behind him, than my friend Tayari Jones—writer, teacher, and world traveler—arrived for a visit. Since she called ahead, I had left a glass of wine at the end of the walk for her. I greeted her with my own glass from the top step of the porch. She hopped out with her own folding chair and settled in for a socially distant visit that lasted two hours. "Next time," she said, "I'll bring the wine." And she will. And maybe Eugene will come through and play his saxophone again or Zeke will read a few pages of his new novel or Chris and Brittney will come by and sing a little Hank Williams.

Or maybe Zeke and I will just go walk Elvis in the park like we do every morning and admire the bright blue of a cloudless Southern sky, and that will be enough. Because that is how we got through the horrible early days and weeks and months of the last epidemic I lived through. We stayed close. We made art. We made love. We celebrated every friendship, every glass of wine, every fleeting, irreplaceable, not-promised-to-you precious moment. We laughed a lot. And we loved each other. We loved each other fiercely. Just like now.

Not Allowed

Tayari Jones

I was born in 1970, two years after Martin Luther King Jr. was martyred in service to civil rights for all Americans. As a child, I reaped the benefits of the sacrifices of my parents' generation. I was spared the tyranny of Dick and Jane, instead learning to read with books featuring drawings of happy, beautiful Black children. My first pediatrician was a Black man, modelling for me and my brother that we could be doctors, scientists, or whatever else we wanted to be. I never felt the sting of a racial slur hurled at my face until I was about forty years old, living in New York City. Because of the strong foundation on which I had been built, I experienced the insult with annoyed disbelief, not as a blow to my soul.

Social justice has always been my parents' ministry. As a mere teenager, my mother participated in the Oklahoma City sit-ins, two years before the famous Greensboro demonstrations. My father protested segregation at the Greyhound bus station; for his trouble, he was arrested, jailed for a week, and then expelled from college. Their bravery was rooted in a commitment to bettering the world for the next generation. This is my parents' greatest gift to me: a life without the daily in-your-face racism that they faced growing up in the Jim Crow South.

But now, in 2020, my parents are on my mind every day, as we are living in a horrific Venn diagram, where the plague of racism overlaps with a global pandemic. Mama and Daddy are, thankfully, in good health. But they are seventy-seven and eighty-four years old. They aren't young any more. Covid-19 is especially dangerous to the elderly. It is especially lethal for elderly Black people.

Luckily, my parents listen to doctors. Daddy is particularly compliant, wearing the masks my mother sews, even when we meet for our weekly outdoor visits.

The conversation inevitably turns to politics, and all of our moods darken. Every day there is another outrage. The police murders are the hardest, as they echo the lynchings that were an omnipresent danger in my father's boyhood in small-town Louisiana. Above his mask, his eyes reflect anger and despair.

My parents live in a lovely neighborhood of roomy stucco homes, nestled on cul-de-sac blocks, adorned with crepe myrtle trees and dogwoods. It must be said that it is a lovely Black neighborhood. (The mayor herself lives only a mile or so away.) They chose to live on this side of town because they enjoy the comfort of other Black folks. Here, they are free of the hassles of everyday racism, like your neighbors mistaking your kids for prowlers and calling the police. They do, however, have to deal with the soft racism that shows itself in the little things. For example, their favorite grocery chain won't deliver to their home, but pick-up service is an option. I live about fifteen minutes away in an integrated neighborhood, so we have the food delivered to me and then I take it to them. I am happy to be useful.

The person who delivers the groceries also does the shopping. My order appears on her phone and she texts me to ask if it's okay to substitute white rice for brown, or pears for apples. She apologizes that there is no yeast in the store at all. The hired shopper is almost always a Black person, usually a woman. One day, she drove up as I waited on my deck. From my perch, I told her to make sure to take the envelope tacked to the door, where I leave extra tip money. I asked her if she would like a bottle of water.

"No, ma'am," she said. "We have plenty in the car." Unmasked, chatty, and vivacious, she explained that every day she drove two hours to Atlanta. Her town, she said, didn't need much grocery delivery. "Also, we drive for Uber Eats!"

Confused, I said, "Who is 'we'? Do you work with a partner?"

"No! It's me and him." She went to her car and opened the back door. A few seconds later, she showed me a plump baby. She held his arm and bobbed it so it looked like he was waving.

On the drive to my parents, all I could think about was that baby. The delivery woman, an "essential worker," works for low wages and is unable to shelter at home to hide from the virus. I imagined her walking through the store, infant on her hip, shouldering the risk for me and my family. I thought of the extra tip tucked in an envelope. It wasn't enough. It could never be enough.

When I arrived at my parents' home, they were waiting on the lawn, sitting on folding chairs. Daddy stood and took a step toward me, his arms extended, but then he remembered and let them fall to his side. My mother invited me to look at her flowerbeds, fretting that her begonias weren't thriving this year.

I told them about the delivery woman and her baby.

"How old?" my mother asked.

"Six months, looked like."

Daddy frowned at his fist. "This goddamned country," he said.

Now it was my turn to move in his direction, arms outstretched, only to turn away because, in the age of Covid-19, touching is not allowed.

Poem Beginning in the Market as a Meditation on Hope and Fear

Sharan Strange

So what if I have secret crushes on the Brothers who handle produce at the market—the Eritrean whose graceful hands make pyramids of tomatoes and avocados, stack carrot bunches and broccoli with such deliberation, humming inwardly it seems, with a radiance that he surely passes on to the food, enlivening it as much as me, his mask of cordiality cracking a bit when our eyes meet, soliciting, I want to believe, candor and warm regard? The Sudanese juice maker behind clear canisters gurgling with gold, green, and red libations— but I want mine fresh, so he gathers and chops, and my eyes follow as he presses the verdant kale and spinach, celery, lemon, apples, ginger—quick fingers almost disappearing with them into the machine—and I'm arrested by longing, lingering to watch such fluid industry, his rapt devotion to craft—the smile he gives me isn't pained, it's genuine. And, what if I want to believe that he knows this is ritual, that I begin my shopping at his station because it sanctifies a portion of my week?

And my students...or the dreadlocked, book-wielding activists in my many cities of comfort, who move like crisp currency in unpolished boots and unself-conscious elegance...all the Sisters and Brothers detached from all but the compass of their art of war, mindful of every exchange in the militant air...the sharp intake of our *combat breathing*...despite the lithe energy of their intellect and purposefulness, what if, in truth, they're canceled *for* their ambition and potential, for their very *being*—being misnamed menace, the algorithms of their Black lives coded dangerous…? *Mi gente, meu povo, pèp mwen an*…babies *and* mothers, children, women, men becoming smoke…amidst new fevers and drownings and old hate, the calculus of our grief growing—*you and I disappearing?*

And so what if I tried to follow the monk home that time—from the bus, where, surreptitiously, he ate his lunch—hand moving in and out of a cotton shoulder sack nestled within the saffron folds of his robe—placing each bite like a heavy stone on his tongue, and swallowing with it the turmoil of the afternoon, leaving peace in his wake…?

If, instead, I followed the urgings of his kind—holy exiles who skirt the edges of my own exile, inhabiting a space I imagine imbued, like the arabesques of old trees, with forms and tones of energy and stillness, an aesthetics of deep awareness—and entered that haven, its primordial atmosphere evoking a keen, animal sense of aliveness that surges in wonder as much as fear…to then emerge, incandescent, embracing my own name's conjure…?

Taking refuge too in ancestors who speak to me through the veil of dream—Miz Harriet Tubman in a multi-hued skirt at the house party in Brooklyn, and my own dear mother, returned home, her face aflame like a peach—or in stories, saying *surrender to the free fall*, and *come alive*, and *it is better to speak*, and *are you sure you want to be well?*

And if I let go, now, the incessant sifting of what might and might not be?—assured, rather, by what I see *true*: each set of dark hands offering up its bright attainments, enticing me this time with a pomegranate's beaded bounty among the heap—jeweled inner self broken open, turned outward to light.

Build Back a Body

Destiny O. Birdsong

Just a few days before beginning to shelter in place during the pandemic in spring 2020, I learned about the Korean concept of *son mat*, which means "the taste of one's hands." It's the complex network of preferences, training, familial traditions, and tendencies (I'm heavy on the salt) that make one's food taste unlike anyone else's. I was at a conference, sitting in a cold convention center with my close friend, Claire, an amazing writer and an equally excellent cook who had recently become interested in the panel's topic: food writing. Neither of us is Korean, but when a panelist, the food writer Noah Cho, described it, we both gasped in recognition. *Son mat* is the thing we're often trying to articulate—when she's describing her grandmother's Puerto Rican fried chicken, or when I'm declaring which mom-and-pop has the best barbecue in town. It's the thing we're supposed to cultivate in order to snag good partners, or the thing that makes my friend Josh's wassail taste like the simmering nectar of the gods.

The truth is that, at least up until now, my hands didn't really have a taste. I'm the child of a mother who cooked often, but rarely taught us about how to do it, and I can't blame her. My mother worked backbreaking jobs throughout my childhood: cafeteria worker, mail sorter at the post office, line worker at a trash bag factory. She also took care of her twin sister, who was disabled, and my sister and I weren't exactly considerate, polite children. (Well, at least not to each other. We still aren't.) My mother's time in the kitchen might have been her few sweaty moments of peace in an otherwise overwhelming day, so, for the most part, she left us out of it. She did, however, conscript us into the rote tasks of holiday cooking: grating pounds of vegetables for cornbread dressing, or shelling (for pies) the pecans she got from family members' trees, since store-bought pecans were outrageously expensive, even in Louisiana, where…they literally grow on trees. My hands would sting on Thanksgiving and Christmas mornings, covered in nicks from absentminded grating or intractable shells, and always smelling faintly of onion, even after a bath. I came into adulthood deeply indifferent about cooking: my favorite dishes tasted best when someone else made them (like Jack in the Box), and the thought of cooking for myself was as unpleasant as the miasma of chives wafting from my childhood knuckles.

And then one day, in my early thirties, I was diagnosed with an autoimmune disease: my body had begun attacking itself by attacking my digestive tract. I have my theories, and if I had to put money on them (and I do, sort of, since I pay out-of-pocket for my health insurance), I'd say this disease is my body's awakening siren. The years before its onset were calendars filled with disaster: there was a rape I couldn't admit happened until a friend told me about hers, and her story felt like she was reading my diary aloud. There was the man in the yellow car who tried to run me off the road in the middle of nowhere, who circled back around to call me "nigger" while I was checking my car for damage, too naive—or perhaps too optimistic—to understand the real danger wasn't something that could be covered by auto insurance.

My body responded to these moments of unforeseen harm with a hypervigilance that invaded every part of my body, down to my viscera, and then traveled up, out, onto my skin. When the doctors who diagnosed my illness prescribed biologics—which are created from living organisms, often using recombinant DNA technology—the medicines unleashed an explosive form of eczema: my hands, legs, and feet erupted into pustules that itched until they burst, taking the outermost layer of me with them. When I complained, the doctors prescribed different ones. It took eighteen months for them to realize that the culprit was a combination of the chemicals I pumped into my thigh once a week and my body's own idiosyncratic way of rejecting them. In the meantime, I lost my hair; my fingernails yellowed and separated from their beds, peeling back like the skin of an orange. My ears filled with fluid. Whenever I complained, I was told to wait. Biologics can be dangerous for many reasons (weakening the immune system is only one of them), but they were prescribed for my eventual good; after all, they'd never done this to anyone my doctor had seen before. My body, Black and woman, was not special. It would eventually adjust. Meanwhile, austere brochures for cancer insurance began arriving in the mail, colored the blues, tans, and whites of the church fans the ladies used to wave during Sunday service back home. The fans were often printed with famous faces, like that of Martin Luther King Jr., on one side, and advertised funeral homes on the other.

So it was no wonder that, even before the pandemic came, I was already so very, very tired of fighting my body's enemies—internal and otherwise. I was so eager to sit in one place and take a breath.

When Claire called for the fifth time after we left San Antonio, where the conference was held, to tell me to stock up on canned goods and dog food, or to just forget all that and head to Nebraska, where she now lives while pursuing her Ph.D., I laughed. And when she said, during one of her many come-to-Jesus (or, rather, go-to-Kroger) conversations, "In case the apocalypse comes, we should also learn how to shoot," I laughed again. And when she added, "Wait, no. Since I can't drive, you can be the driver, and I'll be our protection. I can learn to shoot from the car window," we both laughed, because we are Black and Brown girls who are so vulnerable that such a plan is both heartbreakingly necessary and completely impossible. We aren't safe anywhere, not even at home, but any cop who saw us careening down a flyover-country highway with a semiautomatic hanging out of the passenger window isn't gonna give us a chance to explain why we're running; he's gonna kill us before we can switch lanes. Even so, I pretended to hear her, and I pretended to consider leaving. But I am not leaving. Not because I'm ignorant, or don't believe that the world (at least as we know it) is ending. I'm not listening because I'm too tired to move. I'm too tired of being frantically afraid to die.

Furthermore, the mere mention of stockpiling crackers and ramen, and daily downing soggy green beans and waterlogged chickpeas that taste faintly of metal, curdles my stomach into that familiar gurgle. The thing is, when I eat indiscriminately, I pay dearly, especially now. I've been off all my medicines—the ones that harmed me and the ones that did the work of healing me from that harm—for a year and a half now, opting instead for a more holistic approach to my care: consistent rest; a gluten-, dairy-, and soy-free diet. But even so, I'm notorious for breaking my own rules. Chunks of Gouda. Margherita pizza and gelato. I've eaten a thing again and again, just to make sure it's really forbidden. I know my body can take a repeated mistake. I've done as much to it with so much else—sun exposure, men—patting myself on the back when I come out unscathed. But, on the phone, I make one promise aloud to Claire, and one silently to myself. The first is to head to the store, and the second is to try to "live right" by this quarantine, and see how long I can go without the foods that trigger my symptoms. Unfortunately, some of those foods—bread, real cheese, red wine—are the ones that make life delicious.

Fortunately, one of the gifts of my life is having friends who know how to cook. Joshua, the king of international cuisine, makes Korean spicy noodles that make me tear up, not only from the spice, but because they're just so damn good. Tafisha's mother passed on to her her famous baked macaroni, which I can modify with vegan cheese and nutritional yeast if I so desire (and I'll be honest, some days I don't desire—it's not the same!). And Claire makes oxtail, a dish I loved enough pre-pandemic to drive almost downtown, past the gentrified streets closing in on my alma mater, past the dainty bakeries and coffee shops with tables made from repurposed barn doors, to the Caribbean restaurant in the old farmer's market to pick up a Styrofoam box that leaked gravy onto my passenger floorboard, and that cost me sixteen dollars before the tip. But I am often disappointed by the portions, or the ratio of edible meat to fatty chunks, which I roll around in my mouth until I've sucked off all the flavor, then throw to my occasionally (and eagerly) carnivorous dog.

So, on one of my designated grocery days, Josh and I don

our masks and meet at the international market, the only place to get quality oxtail, as well as dried squid and sweet potato vermicelli. Just across from the meat counter, I pull out my phone in search of a year-old email, one Claire sent while I was ambitiously trying to finish a fiction manuscript and was eating hot bar wings and potato wedges from Publix. I forward it to Josh, and we begin a leisurely and respectfully distant amble through the aisles in search of ingredients, tossing them into each other's baskets when one of us finds them first, and making recommendations to each other for snacks and hot sauces from around the world. It's a way for us to be together, even Claire, who texts her encouragement as I search a shelf crowded with dried herbs, some of which I've never even heard of.

At home, I rub thyme, allspice, and paprika into each disc of meat, still stiff with cold and now gritty with salt. The spices stain my hands, reminding me of a past life, one in which I grated—and ate—with abandon. I let the meat rest (as my mother says) on a scratched yellow plate while I sauté the vegetables. I double-check the recipe, which I have printed and stuck to the refrigerator. "Definitely an onion!" writes Claire. "Definitely garlic! People also put carrots and celery." When I text to tell her I'm building the broth, she writes, "A tablespoon of ketchup and soy sauce go a long way to deepen the flavor." I fish out a few packets from old takeout and measure them in. "Enjoy, my love," ends the email. The rising steam and the memory of her voice with its Staten Island swagger warm my face, and I smile into the pot before I cover it. In the next few hours, the air thickens with flavor, like the gravy, and halfway through hour three, when I taste it to see if I should add more liquid or salt, the first note is rich with thyme, but has a sweet finish, a phrase I learned from Josh one night as he freestyled a cocktail by mixing sugar-free energy drinks with cucumber-flavored vodka.

Have you ever bitten into something that tastes like love? Or like home? Like the smell of red dirt and pine trees and Sundays when your mother put beef-tips in the crockpot, and shuffled you off to church in your itchy stockings with your hair glistening with Blue Magic, and you come home sweaty, either from the Holy Ghost or from riding in a car with no air-conditioning, and you have the whole afternoon ahead of you, so you change into your play clothes while your mother moves around in the kitchen, clanging pots and pans? If she's soon distracted in another room—maybe taking care of your aunt—you have just enough time to sneak into the kitchen and slip a slice of white bread from the bagged loaf, the Sunbeam girl grinning at you from the crinkled plastic as you retwist the tie. Then carefully, and without clattering it, you lift the lid from the crockpot and dip the slice of bread into the gravy, because dinner will be served soon and all you need is a little taste. It's like touching the hem of a rich garment. And maybe the hem of the garment is what human love is: flustered sometimes, yes, and flawed, but adjacent to the Divine, made by hands that will one day die, but took time out of their allotted years to make a meal that fills you with something that will keep you alive.

Now, imagine an older you, marked by time and tragedy, whittled into a sharper version of your girl self, who has the whole pot to herself: no sharing with aunt or sister, no Mama hovering, doling out the portions so they last. Everything is yours, and you can have it whenever you want. That's what I taste when I slide a morsel of homemade oxtail from my fork, and the meat and the fat and the meaty fat dissolve in my mouth. Oxtail is one of those dishes where there's really no right or wrong way to season it (although Jamaicans and Southerners might try to convince you otherwise), so the only thing I can tell you is that when someone makes it for you, or when *you* make it, and when you share it or eat it alone, it should make you feel like someone gathered the strength of their hands to make something for you that says *love*. Perhaps they are doing it in a place where oxtail is expensive and hard to find, or they had to go out looking for it in a food desert, or they made it for you because the gentrified restaurant up the street is serving it at thirty bucks a plate and pairing it with some bullshit like elderflower jelly or rice and peas that are literally rice and peas. It's important to remember that oxtail, like chitterlings, like tripe and pig's feet, is a part of the animal that, traditionally, no one wanted. Think of all the hands that grappled with that truth, and then grappled with rendering that meat edible and tender, that meat that was thrown to them and theirs like scraps. When I think of this, I think of the scriptures we were forced to memorize at children's church during those Sunday services, especially the ones about the lengths people go for those they love—like the story of the paralyzed man whose friends brought him to see Jesus in the hope that he'd be healed, but because the house was so crowded, they couldn't get in. In desperation, they lowered him inside through a hole they made in the roof. That's how I feel when I cook and eat food like this, food that doesn't harm me, but facilitates my health. Food that was originally considered the exact opposite of healthy, but that defies those expectations. That's how I feel when my friends show me how to do it.

I feel decadent receiving this kind of love, which I'm lucky enough to have, even now, in my sometimes lonely apartment with the probably racist downstairs neighbor in a city in a state where Black women are dying all the time, even while giving birth—and so are their babies. At the same time, I feel swaddled in this little nest I've made for myself, cut off by miles and singlehood and the familial estrangements that have made impossible the tactile togetherness some folks are now desperate to escape. I've certainly been loved through food before; my mother cooked for us, and often made food choices (like skim milk and ground turkey) that were designed to gear us toward health. But now there are limitations on that love. My mother, who makes the annual declaration that she's outdone herself with this year's sweet potato pie or gumbo, can't make a moist gluten free cake to save her life. But every year, a week after Christmas, she tries, because the thought of me baking my own birthday cake is an insult. I eat her uncharacteristically dry-ass cake and say nothing. She has always done the cooking, and doing it now is a way to love me whenever I am close by.

However, I've never been loved through the sharing of cooking in a way that empowers me to make food on my own until now, when it has become one of the many iterations of my relationship with Josh and Claire during shutdown. We trade photos of what we make: "Hot pepper peach japchae!" boasts Josh in the group chat, captioning an exquisite photo of a benoodled bowl garnished with what might be Thai basil (like I said, I'm still learning). Claire sends a photo of her garden, vowing to plant mint to keep the squirrels away. The next time I make oxtail, I add a jalapeño in absence of the habanero Claire suggested for heat, and later, I use leftover peppers to make hand-breaded poppers stuffed with vegan cheese spread (eat your heart out, Jack in the Box). I also try my hand with Josh's noodles, throwing in whatever I have on hand: shrimp and egg and spinach. "Girl, that makes you a cook!" replies Claire when I send a photo. "When you start to improvise like that, that is the mark of a cook."

I grin and look around my apartment. Everything in here is improvised, including my life. When I lost my job last year, I decided that, for as long as I could, I would only do work that brought me joy: writing, talking about writing, reading, editing, teaching writing at a local co-op, and occasionally making stuff around the house. The month after leaving work, I took one look at my peeling leather couch and said, *Yellow velvet pillows would be nice.* So I made them as a replacement for the back cushions, and covered the seats with red slip-covers, buying a teal carpet to (not really) match. The new decor jibes perfectly with a Xavier Payne print above the fire-place: it's a scene from my favorite sitcom, *Martin*, where the eponymous star fumes in the foreground while his girlfriend's bestie, Pam, taunts him, her hand held high like a matador. His best friends Tommy and Cole look on, while Brother Man rifles through the fridge in the background. Every inch of that scene is awash in the ROYGBIV palette of my childhood, the nineties, the last decade I remember being as happy as I am in this one. I've let those colors bleed into the rest of the room, and it has become my most favorite place I've ever lived. This is further bolstered by the screened-in porch with an enor-mous beanbag chair that I paid another writer for with copies of two poetry anthologies in which I was featured. I spend quiet mornings on it, sipping decaf chai with coconut milk while journaling, as the evergreens that canopy my corner of the building shimmer under the weight of squirrels leaping between them, and the wild geese that populate the apartment complex's lake honk and chase each other in the distance.

Here, I think sometimes of Mary Oliver, who thought about things I rarely put in poems, like geese, and who wrote so simply yet so astutely about the world around her. One of her most famous poems, "The Summer Day," is, among other things, about a grasshopper eating sugar from the palm of the poet's hand, her strange jaws working it down in her own way. *That's me*, I think to myself: I'm figuring it out as I go (see Lucille Clifton), eating from generous hands, washing my eczema-free face at the end of each day, a ritual that is its own prayer. I know that I am, like they say, *safer* at home, but only marginally so. I'm part of a demographic predisposed, according to numerous studies, to dying first and fastest. I might develop a cough tomorrow and a doctor could take one look at my BMI and decide I'm too "high-risk" to intubate. I might, like Breonna Taylor, be shot to death in my own hallway due to a no-knock warrant served on the wrong house. I think of Tafisha's refrain when we joke about the transgressive things we fantasize about doing in the future: *Who's playing games?* she asks, throwing down the gauntlet. The answer? No one is. Not the cops. Not doctors. Not me. But I am practicing something else: deep quiet and quiet joy. In the last lines of "The Summer Day," Oliver asks: "Tell me, what is it you plan to do / with your one wild and precious life?" I'm pretty sure that when she wrote it, she wasn't thinking of a Black girl filled with mercurial white blood cells living in a red state who is just now learning to love herself one bite of nourishing food at a time. But I don't care. I'll use whatever I can to survive. That's me not playing games.

Because the truth of the matter is, no matter how many laps I make around the lake, watching the deer watch me across the algae-thick water, or marveling as a blue heron dips into seamless flight, this is not a vacation. It's a readying for battle. Every morsel I eat, every step I clock around the complex is a calculated attempt to improve my chances. I have come to treat my body like the food I prepare: perishable and precious. I'm careful when making oxtail because my budget is thin, and oxtail is too expensive to screw up. I have to keep that same energy with myself. So I pay attention. I want to come out of this all right. Every day, I head to the fridge, spooking the dog by pulling its heavy door toward her, because she's not supposed to be in my kitchen anyway. I stare for a minute, then start fishing for what's inside, my palate inspired, my instincts sharp, my hands itching to season.

Feasting on Bread and Dry Bones

Shay Youngblood

On March 13, 2020, the day Covid-19 was declared a national emergency, I was in Philadelphia at the launch party for my first published work in a decade, a graphic novel collaboration featuring a Black woman superhero. It was also the day my spouse of more than ten years told me she wanted to divorce. A few weeks later, I would move again for the third time in less than two years.

In the first chapter of the pandemic, I ended up sheltering-in-place alone in my new home in the Old Fourth Ward in Atlanta, where cooking would become part of my daily practice as an artist. I filled my pantry, my freezer, and a hall closet with enough food and supplies to last for months. Two shelves of one kitchen cabinet brimmed with spices from around the world. My kitchen transformed into a creative lab, a room in my memory palace, a place of comfort in unsettling times.

My new home in a rapidly gentrifying neighborhood was

close enough to walk to four large chain grocery stores. Those walks became my daily exercise. I used the *New York Times* section "What to Cook This Week" as my guide to create dinners for one. While friends and family were taking online classes in yoga, concealed weapons, and Sanskrit, I cooked three meals a day plus snacks, seven days a week.

A lot of things comfort me in hard times—music, art, friends, family, nature. In one day, I streamed the *Nixon in China* opera, took a playwriting master class with Suzan-Lori Parks, had a virtual dance-off with a friend in Texas, and attended a surprise Zoom birthday party for which I dressed up and then raised a glass of champagne in an empty room. Yet food, most of all, is what has eased my anxiety during the most challenging periods of my life.

On the first morning of the lockdown, I headed out early. I turned onto a usually busy main street. Few cars were on the road, and for more than seven blocks I didn't pass a single person. I arrived at the grocery, put on my required mask, and wiped down my cart. The air in the grocery store was thick with the feeling of panic and fear. The morning news showed empty shelves, which fueled my concern that staples might be unavailable.

It felt dangerous to have left the house without a shopping list. What I did have was an insatiable hunger for things from my childhood—like cherry Jell-O, sardines, peanut butter, collard greens, fried chicken, cornbread, vanilla wafers to make banana pudding, a bacon and jelly sandwich on white bread. I imagined that being stuck inside, I'd have time to experiment with recipes, so I loaded my cart with dozens of spices and condiments. In one month, I spent seven hundred dollars on groceries. I didn't order takeout even once.

When I craved Indian food, I looked up a recipe and went to my pantry to create dishes that made me cry. I baked cookies just for the aroma. I discovered that I could make up a batch of ginger and cinnamon-spice oatmeal cookies and freeze the dough into a log so I'd have fresh-baked cookies whenever I wanted. I went around the world in my kitchen, reaching for comfort and distraction in quick Japanese pickles, Spanish omelets, BBQ tacos made with jackfruit—and stews, the delicious stews. I experimented with old favorites, plating my meals in gorgeous Instagram-worthy arrangements on fancy dishes and serving myself champagne or mineral water in gold-rimmed crystal glasses. When I craved meat, I made oxtail stew with thyme and a good red wine for gravy that I sopped up with a thick slice of bread.

One afternoon, I looked out of my office window and noticed a young Black man walking along the back fence outside my duplex. His thick Afro looked dusty, slept on, uncombed. He was shirtless, his chest lean and dark brown. With sagging jeans two sizes too big, a dirty white blanket around his shoulders like a superhero cape, he cut across the grassy lot behind my house and approached the large blue dumpster assigned to the apartment building next door. I watched as the young man circled the dumpster. He reached in and pulled garbage bags out, dropping them at his bare feet. He leaned over the small pile, tore open the bags, and poked through them. I thought he might be looking for bottles or cans to sell. Times are hard, I thought. I turned back to my computer but kept thinking about him. When I looked again, he was sitting on the ground with his back against the dumpster. I watched in horror and fascination as the young man ate food he pulled from a garbage bag in the middle of a pandemic. He chewed and swallowed each bite as if savoring a restaurant meal. My stomach lurched, and my eyes filled with tears as I looked away, paralyzed in my spot by the window. A few moments later, he was gone. I felt a sting of shame. Why hadn't I offered the hungry man a meal from my own well-stocked pantry, itself an embarrassment of riches, a trip through time back to the desires of my youth? Having experienced housing insecurity, I know it is a privilege to be able to turn to my art, to the writing of this essay, to reckon with the heartache I feel for this man. I know that it is not enough.

That night, I had a dream—a nightmare really—that I was homeless, dressed in dirty clothes, coughing, wiping away sweat from my face as I pushed a shopping cart full of cans and bottles. I was living on the street, afraid that I would soon be desperate enough to eat out of a garbage can.

It was day 223 of the pandemic, according to my journal, when I had another dream. In this one, I walked to the grocery store. It was a beautiful spring day. The sun was shining in a cloudless sky, birds were singing, and a gentle breeze caused the leaves to sway as if they were dancing. The streets were nearly empty. On my short walk, I passed only four or five people on the sidewalk. The few cars on the street sped by as if being chased by the virus. When I reached the store, about a dozen people wearing masks of every color and kind were lined up one body length apart. At the head of the line, a young man wearing a yellow-flowered apron, pale blue mask, and lavender gloves sprayed my hands with sanitizer. A presanitized, shiny red cart was positioned in front of me. I pushed the cart forward, hoping there would be something left on the shelves to fill it. There were expensive cans of crab meat, cheap black bottles of no-name champagne, and large tubs of fancy nut butters. There were limits on essentials: three dozen eggs and one package of toilet paper per person, if available. The aisles were full of people who looked stunned, like they'd been hit with a beam of light. Their eyes were stretched wide, and they walked slowly as if underwater. Their fingers twitched as if signing signals of distress. I pushed my cart slowly and kept my distance from the other shoppers.

When I turned down the paper products aisle, I saw a teenager standing in front of the empty shelves. She was not wearing a mask despite the rule. Her black cloth mask hung around her neck, its ties trailing down her chest. Her hair was a huge halo of dark curls sprinkled with glitter. The cloud of hair framed a pretty brown face on top of a thick frame in a body-hugging blue-jean jumpsuit. She smacked on a wad of gum in her right cheek. She pressed her lips together and blew a pink, sparkly bubble that trembled as it stretched bigger and bigger and bigger until it grew to the size of her Afro. When it popped, she smiled and sucked the sticky wad back into her mouth. "Nothing lasts forever," she said. When she noticed me standing the requisite six feet away, her eyes landed on me warily. She reached for a roll of toilet paper—there was none, all of it having been ransacked by panicky shoppers—but still she pantomimed the motions of lifting a package off the shelf and dropping the invisible rolls in her basket, already filled with several cans of crab meat, bottles of champagne, and a tub of cashew butter. I watched her stroll down the aisle with a giggle in her walk.

A few weeks later, in the waking world, a single tent popped up on an empty corner lot across from my house. Soon, there were five tents, and then there were a dozen people living on the land. I rarely saw anyone enter or leave the tents during the day, but at night I saw the glow of a computer screen in one tent and watched the single garbage can in the center of the area fill up and spill over onto the ground.

A year into the pandemic, a young, gaunt white woman in a black hoodie and sturdy boots, pants hanging off her small frame, strolled down the driveway next to my house and approached the big blue dumpster. She disappeared inside and came out a few minutes later with clothes over her arm. Moments later, I heard noise under my deck. The following day, I noticed that plastic bags inside my garbage can had been torn open. Anyone looking in my trash would find only ripped up drafts of false starts on a new novel, letters I never sent, stale bread and dry bones. There must be more I could do, I thought, than donate to the local food pantry.

In June 2021, I walked into a grocery store, wearing a mask as usual, and heard an announcement that people who had been vaccinated were free to remove theirs. I felt a sense of elation. As the world slowly opens up, it means that I can look forward to sitting down at a table with friends and family to laugh and feast together. It means traveling again to places that will feed my imagination and bring new recipes and food memories back to my home kitchen. Yet I can't help but think of all the people for whom there will be no feasts. No new recipes.

In my last vivid dream, I invent a bright yellow pot that is always filled with delicious, healthy comfort food. No matter how many people eat from it, the pot is never empty.

Spring Mix

Opal Moore

for Ahmaud

1.
A small bird built a secret nest
beneath my balcony. There must be
hatchlings there out of view.
She flies back and forth, small prey
in her beak.

Some kind of wren, I think.
Small, brown, and quick. No time for
singing midday. Duty
is her instinct.

She flits. Frets. Undeterred.
She knows the world as it is. No
conspiracy, no theory. Life, for her,
is life. Open throats and beak. Trust,
her leaving marked by each return.

2.
My neighborhood is gentrifying.
The whites are here, folks say.
We will get sidewalks now. And four-way
stop signs at the corner where that grandma
and her grandbabies were killed that time.

They walk their dogs. Push baby carriages.
Post paranoia on Ring.

I have a Ring doorbell. We watch and
don't subscribe. A gimmick,
my husband says, a veteran. Air Force.
(Not to be confused with Space Force.)
We watch dogs on leashes shit on our lawn.
We watch for property tax hikes.
I watch a jaybird harass
a black and brown cat, her
message: *do not tarry here.*

3.
From my window I watch a carpenter bee
drill a new hole in my front post. NPR
drones on in the background—they do
ads now like news. Across the street a boy plays alone
in his driveway. The virus dictates his solitary game.
Another boy sits in the family car. Doors flung open.
He wears earphones, private dances to House.

My nephew's here today. We
entertain him on the deck. He can't come in,
took a plane from Orlando. Arrives
bearing flowers—spring mix
in a cut glass vase, and a white orchid.
We remember not to hug.

4.
Mother wren is not alone. She has a mate.
To my eye they are indistinguishable male, female.
They flit to and from the nest, tireless

they tend fledgling life. I wonder if they
think that this is hard. I wonder if they mourn
the one among too many mouths
to feed, the one outbid by its siblings, the one
who will fall from the nest, not fly.

I think my springtime thoughts. The wrens
see the world as it is. As it must be—a conspiracy
of need. My husband jokes he will
charge them rent. The gift orchid trembles
white in a breeze unthreatening
as the lithe brown boy jogging
past this house, his daily run
unmolested.

Memorial Day 2021

for George Floyd 2020, the (in)visible man

Something pleading as
taps at dawn

a man negotiates for life, now
on playback   his last breath, now

an archive:

on mobile phone
on body camera, on-

lookers' amygdala   the
first-year anniversary is time

a clock flips digits zero
to nine   a cashier franks a killer to be kind.

*

What does it cost to be kind?
witness your own death, reel

time?   *be apparition of faces*
in a crowd, Black petals like a bough

of sight-filled anguish—
a postcard negative of white joy?

or just a matter of fact: this
is what we have to deal with

nickel & dime change
a spectacle death done

without rope tree gun flame—
pieces of a man will not be distributed.

*

Cup Foods Fresh Meat & Produce
takes no shit nor counterfeit
bills   here you can buy stamps and phone

cards and organic milk   a T-shirt and
halal meat   there's not a tree in sight
on this corner nor grass

or flower pot this scene is concrete
and glass   flashing lights on a cop car
compete with a street light's red yellow green

the officer rests a knee
on a dying man's neck   casually
counting last breaths.

*

Dear invisible man
you are not buried
at Arlington though

some would call you war hero
or is it your death mask so

full of wonder   you

so *seen*:
Invisible Man
you flickered briefly into view

in sparks of expiring magic
you achieved a body
perceptible to the dumb eyes

of the charmless. Out of
this underground of light bulb's visibility
surely   this is not enough.

*

Your dying declaration was a
Mother   pure surrender   dishonored
last breath can linger

in the air
the way sparks spiral
up from a night-lit flame

semi-lethal ash   bits
of threat whisper up
into crisp night air

like shimmering arsonist bugs
teasing the parchment-dry
branch   or a world house to ignite.

Pandemics and Portals:
Listening That Breaks Us Open

Daniel B. Coleman

I spent the first couple of months of the pandemic in an agoraphobic panic. I wore gloves and a mask to my grocery store outings and limited those to once or twice a week, maximum. Since we still did not know enough about how the virus was transmitted, I followed the updated recommendations. So, when I came back from said outings, I would spray down all of my packaged goods and wrapped vegetables with Clorox and then get the paper bags out of the house. I regularly Cloroxed my countertops and all doorknobs that I touch with any frequency. I kept away from everyone. It was just me and my dogs. Then, as more information unfolded, I realized that the level of anxiety I was holding about the situation was (1) not sustainable and (2) not quite as necessary. Still, I did not lower my sanitizing standards and social distancing protocol.

Fast forward to November of 2020. While at a gathering of my spiritual community members in Chicago, one of my beloveds had been infected with Covid and did not know it until we all returned home. I had been so careful until that moment, motivated to risk the gathering by what could only happen by being together in community. I had a sinking feeling that my hypersensitivity would necessarily mean I had contracted the virus.

Though I am young and normatively healthy, I was a sickly child and came down with most every sickness that came through the seasons. I am an HSP, or "highly sensitive person," in mediumship, emotions, and immune system, and as such, I have to think in meticulous detail about how I move through the world and with whom. I was visiting my new partner when I heard the news of my exposure and was devastated about the impact it might have on them and their family, but alas, we were already together. They assured me they knew the risk they were taking, and we waited it out. I took my first Covid test by mail nine days after exposure and it came back negative. I thought I was in the clear. Day fifteen, I began to have congestion and then a fever. I am an asthmatic so I was terrified of the idea of contracting Covid because of the harmful effects it could have on my body. At this point, however, I was still telling myself I had a back spasm and "something else." The next day, I went to an urgent care to receive a cortisone shot and the day after, felt better though I still had a fever. "Not everything is Covid," loved ones assured me.

At four o'clock the next morning, after the shot had worn off, I felt a pain in my back unlike any I had ever felt before. I became almost immobile. I woke up my partner, saying I needed to get to the emergency room. Once we got there, I had to be wheeled in. Walking was unfathomable. I had to wait for some time to be seen. They tested me for Covid again: positive. They gave me medication and sent me home after a couple of hours. The next nine days were a blur. I ate enough to take my medication and go back to bed. The virus skipped my lungs and went for my nervous system. I developed a raging fever and a pain in my lower back so severe that moving, lying, and sitting all made me cry. Lidocaine patches, baths, rubs, and Netflix got me through. My brain stopped feeling like my own. By week three, the pain started to subside and converted to a low, dull ache. I was reminded of the fragility of the body to outside contaminants of all kinds.

At the peak of my feverish days in bed, I started to hallucinate. I saw bright colors and shapes that looked like some of the picture filters on Instagram. I got messages from the virus inside of my body. I listened. It became very clear that this virus is a being, not an "it," as many Western discourses and languages like to classify all that is non-human. It has a spirit. It told me that this is a message from Nature of what is ahead if we do not move in right relationship. It came to humble us and to demand an ecological reorientation. And in this natural order, no one is "special"—it strikes at random to make clear that our relationship with the ecosystem we inhabit is not right and we have a collective responsibility to change it. It decentered all forms of exceptionalism, even as access and exposure mitigated by humans tried to eschew this lesson.

The message is a clear one: it is almost too late. We are exasperated at the longevity of the pandemic, but imagine how much more desperation we would feel after entire countries are submerged under water, food sources running out, potable water dried up or too contaminated by our excess to fuel our water-based bodies. Octavia Butler was right when she said: "There is nothing new under the sun, but there are new suns." Everything we need to know has already been said, has already existed in the Afrofuturist repertoire.

I thanked the spirit of the virus for allowing me this type of access. I needed to get it to receive this message and to share it forward. I thought about how my own book project in this moment begins by addressing how our arguments of natural vs. unnatural, particularly in relation to trans people (being a trans person myself), are some of the greatest hypocrisies of our time. The virus knew I would be one who listened.

I have felt my spiritual capacities growing during and since. Through the peak days of my visual hallucinations, I felt new power come into my hands. During my feverish in-between state of sleep and wakefulness, my hands became portals of ease. I would gently rest my palms on different parts of my body—my face, my belly, my back, my arms—and feel a powerful energy of life and divine gentleness. My own body was pulling me out of it, reminding me that this would end. I never came close to dying from this virus, my body was simply working through it. My channels were opened up in the process. Through sickness, I earned greater access to being able to heal.

In an April 2020 essay in the *Financial Times*, author Arundhati Roy made a declaration that resonated with me and many others. She wrote that pandemics are portals—gateways between worlds that have forced humans throughout history to break with the past.

The novelist added, "We can choose to walk through it, dragging the carcasses of our prejudice and hatred, our avarice, our data banks and dead ideas, our dead rivers and smoky skies behind us. Or we can walk through lightly, with little luggage, ready to imagine another world. And ready to fight for it."

In the portal I fell into during my sickness, I reflected back on the uprisings of the summer of 2020. As Black people, we know that what we carve in the present is an insistence on our brilliance, our art, our imagination, our communities, our cultures, our magnificence, our beauty, and how vanilla the world would be without us. The reality of how we are contemplated as outside of the project of the human has never deterred our joy, our demands for justice, or our work toward thriving.

I watched the news unfold, witnessing the largest demonstrations against racial injustice in the history of this country and remembered that the Civil Rights Movement never ended. I felt so much of everything. My empathic self was on hyperdrive. I wept daily. I yelled. I mourned. I made art. When the opportunity came to march en masse in Greensboro, North Carolina, the city where I live, I knew it was time to mask up and brave the crowd. I needed to feel that collective energy of NO MORE.

In moments of rallying, marching, and protest, when I locate my body within it, all of my senses are heightened. I went alone and took it all in. I did not speak to anyone. There was too much to feel. The electrifying nature of the protest moved like liquid silver through my body. Knots in my throat accumulated as I resisted weeping from the sheer force of the collective emotion. As I marched, I went between chanting and praying (in silence). I prayed for the protection of Olodumare, for the peace and elevation of the fallen ones, for the rejoicing of the ancestors for this collective uprising, for a shield around the protesting body. And I remembered, through my sweaty mask, to *breathe*. Because we can breathe, we can breathe, we *can* breathe.

This portal is also showing us other paths of our destruction. The spirit of the virus moved through like the winds of Oya unveiling and unturning ever hidden nooks of our other collective diseases—white supremacy and corporate greed leading the way. What we have been moving through is nothing less than a reckoning. How do we live with the ongoing terror when ancestral memory reminds us of ways of old? How do we hold generational pain that we did not even experience in our bodies? And then, how can we be good to people within our own communities in the process of liberation? The portal the pandemic opened allowed for a renewal of particular existential questions that ask us to come correct as we face the series of catastrophes of our time.

One product of the uprisings was to hear language that I had formerly only heard in activist spaces in the mouths of the masses. Certainly, this is a blessing and a curse because liberalism and watering down radical and revolutionary thought are not what we want. I have been especially heartened to see and hear all of the ways abolition is now being seen as a framework that can govern every area of our lives, particularly our relationships. The Black love in my life and loving and being loved by other people of color are among my sources of hope. I have spent time inside of this meditation of abolition, finding love in abundance and a much deeper sense of care.

After having felt as sick as I did and all the ways I struggled to keep my online classes going while in feverish hallucinatory states, I was reminded that the system will never give overwork back to us, so I reoriented my priorities. I turned toward my communities, political and spiritual, and I found joy, love, pleasure, abundance, and continued work toward freedom. I deepened my friendships and fell in love. I reinvigorated my profound beliefs in non-normative ways of loving and building kinship. I remembered that I am neither a machine nor a slave and therefore do not have to live as such. I made little shifts to make my home space more beautiful, like purchasing flowers with my food. I deepened my spiritual practice and gave offerings of gratitude for the privilege of having work during this time, without letting work be my life. I prayed to my Egun (ancestors) to let my loved ones be spared.

With the onslaught of devastation, death, turmoil,

degradation, and hatred that we have encountered like the wind of a hurricane bearing down on land, there's one major piece that remains for me. Funnily enough, it came through the lips of Colman Domingo's character Ali in a special episode of the HBO series *Euphoria*. In the episode, Ali tells Rue, played by actress Zendaya, "You've got to believe in the poetry because everything else in your life will fail you, including yourself."

While this message might seem like one of despair, I think there's a more positive message for us here. Poetry—our capacity to continue to search for the divine in the chaos and to use and return to our spiritual technologies—brings in some light. As we call each other out and in, as all that is around us becomes undone, we must find reprieve in the reality of our divine imperfections. We must seek solace in Oya's winds of change. We must find beauty in the system's claim of our unworthiness. We must listen to the elders who already showed us the way. We must remain in the energy of love and care. And perhaps then, we'll find our ways home.

Who to Tell?

Ida Harris

Each visit, I look forward to the banter, the snark, and most of all sitting shoulder to shoulder during a cozy brunch at the Ruby Slipper on Canal Street. This is Black joy. A love I share with my spry, septuagenarian friend. However, this time around, much of it is a no-go. She nixes all that fuzzy love shit on sight.

"Stella, no hug?" I ask, open-armed.

Lovingly she warns: "You stay your Black ass at that distance. Your hug is in the air."

My eyes scan her back office. Shelves that stand as tall as the ceiling are stockpiled with paper towels, toilet paper, Lysol, hand sanitizer, and cases of bottled water.

"Are you serious?" I joke.

"I survived Katrina fifteen years ago, so what do you think?" she snaps.

I live for her snark. I look around. I think about it. I look around again. It clicks. I get it. Survivors consider catastrophes on a whole 'nother level than people who know nothing about catastrophic events. Whispers about a novel coronavirus which began at the top of the year have become hollers by mid-March. The virus poses a fatal threat and is highly contagious. Many people are falling sick and dying. Many others are transitioning to shut-in lifestyles almost ahead of the curve. I digest the seriousness after this conversation with Stella, the owner of Stella Jones Gallery in the heart of New Orleans, where I visited the weekend before shit hit the fan.

I am quarantined from the outside, yet growing nearer to myself and living each day on a rhythmic three-repeat:

> I blink. I yawn. I eat.
> I blink. I yawn. I eat.
> I blink. I yawn. I eat.

I half-ass my way through the remaining coursework the University of Mississippi has transitioned online. The same goes for the three sections of British literature I teach to undergraduate students. They, too, are performing half-assed. This Great Pause has given everyone a legitimate reason to slack, to catch our breaths, to breathe—or so I think. Quite frankly, I am feeling this new-new way—perhaps too much. I'm embarrassed by this sentiment. I am guilty of privilege, selfishness, house-niggering, respite, and security. I have the audacity to experiment with cute recipes that explore Black Indigenous food—pig feet, chitterlings, gumbo—while my loved ones suffer during these ominous times. I want to not hear their challenges, their grief. The fucking nerve of me. How white of me. I grapple with being ain't shit.

A dear friend is spiraling. She don't do well with uncertainty. I am on a high at home working remotely. I'm aight, I think. I read and write headlines for a living. Headlines are her trigger: CORONAVIRUS PREYS ON WHAT TERRIFIES US: DYING ALONE.

"I can't imagine the fear I'd have if I had to die by myself," she says after an overconsumption of trending news.

I recognize her angst. I've known her so long that I feel it. I throw in my two cents because I've been here with her before. A response is necessary.

"Chile, being surrounded by your people at the time of transition ain't some shit that anyone should be denied. Nope, not even in a pandemic."

I remember my dying uncle. He was unwilling to live in a nursing home. He died by choice with my hand in his, my weeping aunt wrapped around him, and Luther Vandross's voice soul-singing in the background. He died a good death. My friend mumbles something about her mom's. "She needed to be there…came off the ventilator…took her last breath." I listen to what she doesn't say because I hear her without hearing. She tells me without telling. She don't do too well with death. Still, we talk at length about shortages and the overwhelming amount of bodies being dropped down in mass graves up in New York City's potter's field. We break into conversation about underwhelming funerals that either cap off at ten people who mourn and memorialize over a closed casket and the funerals that can't go down at all. The homie gets angrier the more we talk about what Covid caused. She fixates mostly on not knowing what she will not know till what she does not know occurs. I tell her to "Clean up, keep house, stay busy." It's all I've got aside from sharing the joys, relief, retreat, optimism, and positivity. I swallow those words. They do not fit the moment. We go on to conspire theories and call out predictions.

"That shit been floating around way before March," I say. "Remember, I was fucked up over the holiday?"

The line is quiet.

"I think I got that shit when I traveled to the Cape."

"Bitch, my whole household was sickly with respiratory issues by the time you returned, and remember, I had pneumonia," she says.

I do—then I actually backtrack to when she had a mysterious bout of pneumonia. It was late October 2019. We spoke briefly over the phone while she was hospitalized. She wheezed and struggled to breathe between sentences till it made no sense to form another.

"This shit gon' fuck up the election. I bet you," she says.

"Chile, it already started."

I read a breaking news headline even though I know I shouldn't: LOUISIANA POSTPONES DEMOCRATIC PRIMARY OVER CORONAVIRUS, THE FIRST STATE TO DO SO.

My very own headlines haunt me and mine(s).

MY COUSIN, AN ESSENTIAL WORKER, RISKS LIFE DRIVING NEW YORK CITY WORKERS TO AND FROM ESSENTIAL DUTIES.

He has chronic asthma and other underlying issues. He texts, "Shit, if I get it, I don't think I will make it." I swallow deep breaths. The air around me is my own.

AIN'T NOTHING GOING ON BUT THE RENT: BILLS STILL GOTTA GET PAID IN A PANDEMIC.

My son has asthma, too. He lives communally with his on-again, off-again girlfriend, his homie and his girlfriend and their two kids. I tell him to stay in, self-quarantine. He tells me he must find a job—like yesterday. I hit send on an email. Attached to it is a six-month old invoice I forgot to submit. It is one of many oversights because my bills are paid. I am not pressed.

#ALLMONEYMATTERS AS COVID CLAIMS CAREERS, COINS, AND SECURITY

Another close friend may be forced to work her job that deals directly with the public or forced into unemployment. She weighs the odds of possibly contracting a lethal virus against survival. She toys with the idea of early retirement. She rethinks the trajectory of her life and her livelihood. I am careful to not ask her shit about her job. She don't wanna talk about it. So we don't. Unless she wants to. She wants to but not really. I definitely do not speak about my work or financial security.

By mid-April, nearly 45,000 Americans had succumbed to Covid-19. The overarching number doesn't reflect that Black folks have died the most. Black, Indigenous, and Latino Americans are being wiped out at a rate that is 2.7 times more than white folks.

BIG MAMA BLAMED FOR POVERTY AND POOR HEALTH. WAS IT THE SUGAR IN THE GRITS OR THE SALT?

The disparity ain't much different from what we know to be true in all other facets of Black life, but this slight hits different. It strikes home more collectively, swiftly, visibly. While many have grown up in poorer communities with family members who suffered diabetes, heart disease, high blood pressure, strokes, and cancers, we are assuaged with watching them decline and die in pieces—bit by bit, limb by limb—in slow motion, all the while under the auspices of shitty health care and neglect. And now this: somebody knew somebody who knew somebody who got Covid or died from

Covid quite expeditiously. Coronavirus struck niggas like the cat-o'-nine-tails, splitting our Black backs, teasing out pain. It, too, lynched us then blamed us for our deaths.

People don't take kindly to being told how not to die. People are truly bugging. Most don't even like gestures. Not a singular act or display. Not masks. Not gloves. Not large red X's duct-taped on store floors, hyper-white outlines, warnings to the public to step the fuck back—at least six feet—while standing in line to check out items. People are out there dying, and still people are dying to get out.

I need soap, smokes, a box of Cheez-Its and a loaf of bread. In this moment, I am people. I think. But maybe not really. I arm myself accordingly to brave the outside. Gloves, mask, sanitizer, and headwear. I adhere to at least twelve feet of social distance, even in this lonely store that serves the surrounding food desert—and its people who hang state flags that bear the symbol that underscores the sign of the times. I am shrouded in three-fourths of cloth. Only my eyes and gloved hands are exposed. They don't like that. Not none of it.

WHITE PEOPLE WILL WHITE WHENEVER, WHEREVER, HOWEVER, ESPECIALLY DURING A DEADLY ASS PANDEMIC.

Two salty alabaster men walk up closely and stand behind me, unmasked and poorly aged by Confederate pride, Marlboros, and Budweiser Light. I speak upward and point downward as one of these men advances toward my field of safe space.

"Yo. You gotta stand back." I raise my palm to ward off this white invasion. This type of entitlement is pervasive. It upsets me and my skinfolk.

The two men are bigly annoyed by my audacity, my presence, that I am suited and booted like a Brooklyn Muslimah, taking up space and interrupting their reckless flow in a back-wood Mississippi Dollar General.

"This is what socialism looks like," one says to the ashy other who responds, "When the good Lord calls, he calls."

I laugh loudly in what I hope sounds like Black ancestor-speak. I am hoping mostly to offend, yet not forgetting that such a free action, such a rebel attitude, is the reason many of them ancestors are dead. It is not lost on me that rebel white folks remain the reason for such a sickly America. Their boots tread on stolen land. Their red pride taints the soil. I purchase my shit and get out. I return home, where it is presumably safe. I think. I plop myself onto the couch and wrack my brain. I push to imagine healthy spaces for Black people.

I push harder to envision a place for Black women. Where might the doulas and Sulas of life exist and resist without the hint of threat looming above their bodies? I come up short, but the couch is long. It hugs the length and the width of me, my full body and all. Arms, legs, belly, brain. I'm aight, I think. Less guilty, perhaps. I like it here. Self-isolation is giving me life—my peoples, not so much. It is everything I need it to be in the moments I need it to be. I need it to last forever.

It don't.

The phone rings. I answer. Dial-a-doctor has replaced medical appointments in this time of Covid. I recognize the voice. It is clinical. The vocal cords are flat and stretched over grave words. It is Tuesday, April 21, 2020. The time is 4:13 p.m. The knot I fingered in my right titty is fibrous tissue and all benign. The not-so-good news is buried deeper in spaces I cannot possibly feel. The cluster of calcifications floating in my breast are the size of a mustard seed and equally ambitious. It is the coldest call, dark, dry. Even drier than the peanut butter I drag across the pumpernickel toast I was fixing to eat. I fold the bread, crush it in the napkin that holds it, and force it into an already overwhelmed Dollar General bag. Its weight stresses an already vulnerable doorknob. The overflow begs my attention as most of the kitchen did for well over a week. I stop cooking and order in when both kitchen sinks can no longer fit another cup, bowl, plate. In seven days, the best and worst-case scenarios take up space in my mind.

MY BREAST CANCER DIAGNOSIS CAME IN THE PANDEMIC. I WANTED MORE THAN A "VIRTUAL HUG."

I lie facedown on a titty table hoisted in the air with my right arm stretched above its shoulder, as that titty dangles through an opening specifically designed for human udders to hang in the balance while a mad scientist extracts tissue from them. It is the fourth biopsy. I feel handled. Perhaps vulnerable livestock might identify with such poking and prodding. The titty feels like it spent the last thirty-two hours being pitched and batted at a baseball range. The bruising, the aching, the throbbing radiate to other parts of the body—my shoulder, my upper arm, my leg. I am fixated with results: invasive ductal carcinoma, ER+, PR+, HER2 negative or positive or something like that. The caller couldn't convey much more. Answering questions is not in their wheelhouse despite asking if I had any more questions. The caller cannot answer how or what, so there's no sense in asking why. *Why* is the quadratic equation of all lines of questioning. It is hard to reconcile, difficult to unpack, even when an answer exists.

WHY DOCTORS ARE LOSING THE PUBLIC'S TRUST

Why? ain't the first thing that comes to mind. It ain't even the second or third. The first is *Who to tell?* The who is far more pressing than the why. *Why me? Why this? Why that?*

don't count when something or someone or some air is trying to get your casket ready.

But who to tell when you ain't ready, when you scared, when you quarantined? Who to tell when your remains remain, not as survivor, but rather, something *other*, that has yet to be ascribed to Black girls who remain despite having some part of them butchered, amputated, maimed, silenced, or deaded with every attempt made on our lives. Who to tell about thriving in fragments? Who to tell when you survive a guillotine yet function under some other set of knives? Who to tell when people who purport to love you show up as machete, axe, and chainsaw? Who to tell when you are tired, scarred, and ashamed, and you want and don't want, and you're living and dying at the same time? If you're a Black girl who performs a first name or a middle name or a last name or mommy or auntie or sister or niece or friend or bae or bitch or hoe or strong or weak or smart or ugly or beautiful then you are no stranger to telling nothing to no one, even during a pandemic.

Haiku

E. Ethelbert Miller

27
sickness in the air
we are afraid of dying
find joy in living

42
light inside the dark
hope is a robin singing
let us find our wings

55
joy in the morning
now is the time to rake leaves
death was yesterday

56
so heavy the wind
the trees are bending again
come rain lift me up

60
early morning walk
it seems the world is still here
black lives still matter

65
the hunting season
black men running in circles
looking for their wings

89
death don't make me cry
here come the saints marching in
lord play your trumpet

97
our world has collapsed
we now dance with the earthquakes
fear is what moves us

Evidence

Some of us will die in the new year.
Death will be new to us.
It will be something we forgot to place
on our things-to-do list.
We will count our days one last time.
We will place them alongside our memories.
We will leave our clothes in the closet.

False Dawn: A Zuihitsu

Khadijah Queen

1.

I collect living things at the end of their lives. Faint, failed. Gift of a rose half-bloomed before having enough. Dried lilac pressed between high-shelved Lispector volume and Alejandra Pizarnik's *Extracting the Stone of Madness*. Late-summer pine cone brushing the spine of Lucille Clifton's *Collected*. Snapped from the vine to save the others—a yellowed philodendron leaf. Was it the lavender incense I burned the nights I couldn't sleep? Did I make a mistake leaving it in water so long? It thrived all year until now. I brought it home from my office when campus closed. Watched the roots deepen their tangle as they lengthened. Maybe I just need to find the right soil for rescue. Rescue, the action, as opposed to miracle, a noun received, which shifts responsibility to some mysterious *else*. I want to behave responsibly in preserving any life, or honoring its end. Hands moving not in sleight, but service.

✳

I place the second philodendron leaf to lose all of its dark onto the writing desk in my bedroom. The yellow—an almost-sick yellow-green, makes me want to paint. I keep saying that, to myself, out loud, on Instagram, trying to make it real. Brushes and watercolors—ochre, alizarin, quinacridone gold, viridian, carmine, lampblack, Payne's gray, Prussian blue tucked in a fabric box. Unused, have they lost their power? What are we made to do? News of empty meat shelves and workers denied protection and whiny Orange County surfers threatening a measured recovery, the health of beloveds. And aren't strangers, too, beloveds? Do we not call each other brother, sister, in certain gatherings?

The virus doesn't choose who is a stranger; we do. Moon through curtain crack: a thin, ambient light.

2.

Artichokes, asparagus, aspens, autumn. I list what I appreciate. Stray notes to triangulate out of haze. On the first day of quarantine, my mother stood next to the patio doors without opening them. Our apartment building, in suburban Colorado, is shaped almost like a honeycomb, with a courtyard in the center. We overlook a fountain, brilliant sky. She said, "The sun got nerve enough to shine."

She'll be eighty-two this year. Rare, now—a hug, smoothing hair in passing, clasping hands.

3.

The times I made banana bread before the pandemic, I forgot to separate wet and dry ingredients before mixing. I'd read the directions once and think I remembered correctly. This time, I read them again because it has been awhile, and realize that, as usual, moving too fast leads to mistakes. To slow down: a daily decision, moment by moment. What else could I have saved from ruin? I exaggerate. What else could I have done correctly? I think of joy as well as loss—missed taste, lighter texture. I think about the poems I wrote out of rage and despair, bound in a book with a beautiful cover, wonder if I crafted them to fall apart.

4.

In New York, my younger sister has a fever. She doesn't often get sick, and she is so tired she cannot get up without vertigo spinning her back down. On FaceTime, her children climb all over her, pull her arms, snuggle into her neck, touch the outside of her mask. She is too weak and out of breath to stop them. She coughs. I beg her to get the test. I beg her to rest. I beg my brother-in-law to stop working and help her with the kids. He won't. My sister gave up a career in real estate so he could build his. My mother wants to bring the kids here, but she and my sister aren't even speaking. I yell at my mother to fix it, beg her to apologize. She won't.

I bought a hooded Tyvek suit in early March, after Naomi Campbell posted a video wearing one. It takes all my strength not to pack it up and drive across six states to the epicenter.

5.

Lemon balm tea, raw honey, vegan toast, blackberries. White bean soup with carrots, parsley, white pepper and black pepper.

End of week, May 3, 2020: 843 deaths in Colorado. In my county, +20.4 percent from last week.

Legionnaires' disease can travel through air-conditioning vents, my son discovers. He is a gamer, and likes to keep track of rules and facts. The largest outbreak of Legionnaires' in New York City's history, in the South Bronx in 2015, was spread by cooling towers. The warmer it gets, the less use these ceiling fans will be.

Masked up, glasses on, hair covered by hood or the black Goorin Brothers hat I bought in California with my friend Ariel—I drive to Firestone, Frederick, Longmont, Erie; bring paper booties, gloves, sanitizer, wipes. In the middle of this chaos, I am trying to buy a house.

6.

March and April event cancellations come fraught, swift. I cancel my trip to San Antonio, to appear on scholarly panels and meet up with poet friends I only see once a year. I cancel a vacation in Charleston with my sister, her first since the kids were born. I postpone a weekend getaway to Santa Fe with new friends—not writers, business owners—fellow fans of spas and French food. Took my whole life to allow such pleasures. Rescheduling? Indefinite. Then May, June, July events—poof. Thousands in summer honoraria blink into 2021 or full disappearance. I return clothes I bought for performances while I still can. The line at Nordstrom Rack stretches so far they rope us off in an L shape from the front of the store all the way to the back. Fourth of March. I am the only one wearing gloves and a mask. The cashier has a pump bottle of sanitizer next to the register, but he doesn't use it.

7.

My people are dying at exponential rates. My people are dying. My people. I think about access, influence, screening, separation. The Rona is a monster. Another invisible force that wants to use us up until we die.

A history I spent a lifetime learning flashes through me every time I hear that, as usual, our rate of death is out of proportion with our numbers in the population. I think about the commoditized spectacle of Black suffering that Dr. Saidiya Hartman describes in *Scenes of Subjection: Terror, Slavery, and Self-Making in Nineteenth-Century America*, and I refuse to contribute. I think about the irony of Debord's *The Society of the Spectacle*. I think about the Barthes essay "The World of Wrestling" and how much I used to love the old WWF, the days of Junkyard Dog and Hulk Hogan and Rowdy Roddy Piper. I think about Piper's 1988 film *They Live*, a sci-fi fable about class conflict. I want people to do their own work of understanding, because otherwise they won't understand, ever, and nothing we say or make or do or survive or don't will change it. Absurdly, Jennifer Aniston's line in the movie *The Break-Up* pops into my head: "I want you to *want* to do the dishes."

I cannot write about the police and vigilantes killing us, headlines repeating carceral absurdities that say it's our fault for running, eating, driving, talking, sleeping, existing.

Very tiresome things: victim-blaming; absence of reparations; the constant surprise.

A story blinks nonstop in my Twitter feed in May: a man in Flint, a security guard at a Family Dollar, killed in anger. The rage source: the killer's sister being told to wear a mask. His nickname was Duper, short for Super Duper. His eight children, his mother, his wife, and family and friends shattered into mourning, embracing in masks, weeping. There's a sea of Mylar balloons and lit candles. Every loss: incalculable.

8.

Asthma and other chronic health issues keep both my son and my mother at risk; my mother takes so much medication we have an Excel spreadsheet to keep track. They've sheltered in place for eight weeks. I'm at risk, too, but I try not to think about it. I have to be the one going out. I have to be the one who works, even if I work at home. I record lectures for my students, answer their emails, respond to their poems and essays and questions, try to remain a stable and generous presence for them as the world shuts down.

One of my nieces calls to ask about our heritage—names, places, and dates of birth and death. My mother tells me a story. Fighting snow, looking for a job in Detroit, my grandmother's mother contracted the flu, then pneumonia. A hundred years ago, she died.

9.

March 31: the peak day for deaths in France. 7,578 souls counted. I vault into memories of our summer last year in Paris, Lyon, Arles, Rouen. My son and I have become those people who talk about France all the time, missing the luxe contrast of traveling during an unprecedented heat wave, the ease of our existence there—no suspicion during our exploratory walks and Kapten rides, no feeling of being unwelcome in shops, and plenty of unexpected kindness.

We planned to go back in winter, spill into crisp Côte d'Azur light again. I wanted to visit Baldwin's home in Saint-Paul-de-Vence and go inside, not just touch the wooden door. But we don't know any when or where anymore. My anxiety infuses tweets, texts, calls, trips to the store for more food and supplies. I can't worry about how I look to my colleagues—that would make it worse. More panic attacks in a month than I've had over the past four years. I worry about people being tired of me, but worry more about the risk of disconnection. Early in lockdown, back-to-back, three writers lost to suicide.

One text thread with friends is called "Holy fuck."

10.

Afternoon palimpsest of thought—feels foolish to think about what I make, when I can't help my baby sister. A text from Emily, whose husband works in a hospital, confirms my sister's doing everything right: sleeps on her side, eats healthy, takes vitamin C. One new thing she shares: move as much as you can. On CNN, virus-caught anchor Chris Cuomo said from his basement, "The virus wants us to lie down." He said, "The beast comes at night." Before the pandemic, his corny catchphrases made me roll my eyes. I didn't watch his show. All of April, his segments riveted—human stories that left me weeping. I couldn't write a word.

Pieces of my dissertation got published in *futurefeed*, but it felt strange to share them. A piece of my Navy memoir, from my time as a sailor in the 1990s. Travel diary excerpts— outraged observations of empire in Europe, balanced with rhapsodic musings about the food. And an academic essay.

When I wrote that essay, about the value of studying Muriel Rukeyser even though, like Whitman and Melville—writers she identifies as American literature's light and dark forces, respectively—she operated from a baseline assumption of white supremacy, I meant to provide practical guidelines for analyzing older American literature, for understanding it with greater accuracy, for tracing its cultural influence and mining its prescience. I meant to offer an alternative solution to throwing it all away. I meant to create a means of redefining the canon. Even the intention behind the effort feels like failure. We already live the truth of what and who gets tossed aside.

1:10 p.m., May 3, 2020—a time of reckoning. And 68,040 Americans dead. Around the world: 228,504 people. I hate when reports round up or down. Count every one. Keep counting.

11.

Raise the blinds to let in sun. Group texts and Zoom meetings and emails, the endless electronic scroll zapping my fingers and wrists into a soft curve, tense knuckle peaks, pushing my shoulders tight. My mother writes a note in cursive, for me to pass along to my sister:

> *Another option:*
> *the children can*
> *come here, and*
> *Irshaad's the weekend*
> *Just a thought*

Irshaad is my brother-in-law's brother, and he moved here to Colorado last fall. My sister wanted to come, too, after they visited last summer and loved it, but her husband's businesses are on the East Coast. He refused.

Used to be I could rest through fibromyalgia flares, recover. Now I depend on balms and pills to keep going through the pain. Dr. Bob's, vapor rub, Papa Rozier balm, Aleve PM, Benadryl, charcoal bath salts, lavender oil. Make a pleasure of coffee or espresso for the fatigue. Bless Nespresso machines. Elvazio, Melozio, Hazelino, Voltesso. Solelio for something lighter, if I have to wake up but know I'll need sleep later.

LOL sleep. For the first two weeks of lockdown, I dream about nothing but death. Six nights of scorpions, six of snakes, two of sheer bloody violence—both mass and intimate. Then I wake to press conferences as propaganda, terrifyingly absurd.

All my limbs stiffen overnight. How I wake: slow, scrolling.

12.

Putting on a face is not difficult, because I know who I am.

Let me clarify. I know who I am, but I know how to mask up too.

I'm in meeting after meeting trying not to count faces in squares, track who disappears, each avatar switch, institutional tics. Evening light dominates the room. I like to keep the windows open, but my son fears the virus could travel in on a cough or sneeze. I've avoided my spring-dusted patio for days, and my sister has tested negative. She tested negative, but she's still sick. Negative for flu A, negative for flu B, negative for Covid-19. The coronavirus is a lethal fog of unknowns. "Act like you have it," advised the doctor. "Twenty percent error rate. False negative. Mild case." Or is it something else, not the virus—Google says her symptoms match Ménière's, but I worry about slippery self-diagnoses and informed assumptions. And even if she does feel better soon, if it is the virus, what if it comes back?

For mood lifts, I watch the video my sister sent of the kids singing Kendrick Lamar's "Alright." She's teaching them to say *gon'*. In their sweet and tiny voices, they keep saying, "We're going. We're going to be alright." I smile. My sister has them repeat after her: *moan, bone, gon'*. They laugh. *We're gonna be alright.* Her husband is from Suriname. He says, "We're gonna whaaat?" They can't say it until the end. I laugh every time. I sing it too.

A few weeks later, I text a haiku that makes my sister press the haha reaction:

> *In my sister's yard,*
> *Great horned owls perch in who-song*
> *Soon, murder hornets*

We share the living room by sitting in separate places, at least six feet apart—my mother, my son, and me. Today I notice we are lined up, as if next to each other. One, two, three.

13.

My extended family in Michigan: lab techs, nurses, cleaners. My niece is an LPN at a senior care home where two patients have died of Covid-19. No hazard pay, no PPE. She takes care of her mom—my oldest sister, who had a heart attack last summer, the sister who listens to me read my poems in early drafts, the one who said, when I explained the zuihitsu form: "It sounds like a theater of the mind." I beg her not to go out; she says she's protected—mask, gloves, hat, glasses. But no one else at the laundromat or grocery store does the same. They cough, and don't care who inhales it.

April 30: Men in masks line up on the steps of the Michigan capitol, armed with assault weapons and whiteness, scream about their freedom and call it a protest.

I could preach myself out of breath.

I think about Brecht and Beckett. I think about Fanon and Baudrillard. I think about bell hooks: "There can be no love without justice."

14.

Between cooking and checking on her cousin Nita in Detroit, my mother remembers and corrects memory, talking through Alzheimer's and time collapse: "I remember the Depression. We had these little red tokens, had to stand in a line to get food. Papa didn't even try to work. He just gave up." Papa was her grandfather, not her father, who shoveled coal in Ford's furnace rooms.

Since 2016, I've been writing fables based on my family's history in America, the South and the North, the many violences underneath the various ways of giving up; the riddles my grandfather was known for, how he could play the piano by ear, any song; how his mother escaped a sharecropper's life in Georgia, boarding a train to Detroit with her seven sons, running numbers and taking in laundry in Black Bottom to feed them; the silences of mothers and aunts broken only by my persistent digging. The reimagining is slow because of the pain. I want it honored, but I don't want to make it a parade.

My mother interrupts me with stories while I write and grade papers. She talks so much I have to hole up in my room if I want quiet. On days I listen, I never know if it'll be a story I've heard a million times or something entirely new to me. I love hearing the ones about the garden she had as a child. She tells me what she planted with her father's mother, Rosa, behind the little brick house her father built with his six brothers. Mom stands in the doorway in the one-size-fits-all linen dress I bought for her in Florence, sun on her white hair, and lists a bounty—corn, tomatoes, cucumbers, carrots, cabbage, mustards and turnips and collard greens, okra, string beans, and hot peppers. I ask about the animals. She likes to tell the story of why her sister Evelyn hates chicken: "Gramma would catch a chicken by the neck and *pop*! Lay that chicken on a stump and chop that head right off. Poor thing kept running till it fell in the dirt. Then we had to boil it and pluck the feathers. Evelyn hated the blood, hated that boiled chicken smell." My mom chuckles. "Didn't bother me none." Evelyn became a nurse.

I think of all the families now without parents, siblings, aunts, uncles, grandparents, children, cousins: the devastation will carry over generations. I think of them dying alone, mediated by electronics, and left on a reefer truck until…when? What is the signal for unending grief?

A friend who lives near Elmhurst Hospital describes the ambulance wails as nonstop. Central Park on the first Sunday in May: a Seurat painting, virus-pixelated air, whitely surreal, a false dawn.

15.

What do we face now? What if we fail to protect each other? Miscellaneous questions bombard me. I did so much work to ease my rage, then to rectify a traumatized passivity; what if either comes back? Did I ever believe I was free? Did I ever believe I could pretend not to be?

My uselessness outside the cocoons of home and work feels endless. Then I return to *The Source of Self-Regard*—the only Toni Morrison work I have yet to finish. One chapter and I'm unfooled again.

Deceptive things: healing, archives, talk of inclusion, literary theories, second-dinner hunger, the interruptions of children, trending Twitter topics, the virus.

One Thursday the robins flooded my morning. American, orange-breasted on bare branches, aiming for the light behind thin clouds.

I find out philodendrons need indirect sun. I move this living thing closer into shadow.

Joyride

Karen Good Marable

We're driving east on Boulevard—my daughter and I—windows down, music loud, masks off, feeling free. *Aye aye aye aye!* Swae Lee sings on "Sunflower" from *Spider-Man: Into the Spider-Verse*, one of her favorite movies. Bobbing our heads, we croon right along with him: *Ooooo ooooo oooo ooooooo*. Babygirl is in her booster seat clutching a fatsia leaf with both her hands. The frond is grand and green, the largest on the bush in our front yard. For days, she's campaigned to cut the leaf as only a determined five-year-old Virgo child can, promising to decorate it. Today, said leaf is a flag she's holding out the window, a banner whipping in the wind as we smooth through the A, past the King Center, past Oakland Cemetery, past Zoo Atlanta, on toward Baker Dude Bakery Café where we will pick up Snickerdoodle-Doo cupcakes for tomorrow's pre-K graduation car parade. "Don't you let that leaf go!" I warn, though my daughter's joy is so buoyant, so palpable, it's worth the risk. She squeals from the backseat, "Yaaaayyyy!" laughing, face to the sun, kicking her now-bare feet. My heart grows two sizes and I turn the music up, driving slow enough for her to keep hold of the leaf, but fast enough that we feel like rebels.

Even if we gotta risk it all right now…

These joyrides have become a ritual, a bit of unexpected beauty, in the midst of a global pandemic (where one must be still) and a global protest (where one must take to the streets). As of today's journey, our family has been in quarantine for more than a hundred days. Summer camp plans have fallen by the wayside, much like those color-coded homeschool schedules parents passed around, back when we thought this would all be over in a few weeks. In its place are daily, sometimes pitiful, efforts by my husband and me to educate our kid, get our own work done, love one another, and stay alive. This shelter-in-place sameness was beginning to feel a little like *Groundhog Day*—that is until late winter, early spring when death came in threes.

The back-to-back-to-back murders of Ahmaud Arbery, Breonna Taylor, and George Floyd—unarmed Black people killed by police and white vigilantes policing Black bodies—recalled the bloody summer of 2016 when Philando Castile in Minnesota and Alton Sterling in Louisiana were killed by police within a day of each other. Both executions were caught on video and played on 24-hour news cycles. The difference is that this time, the world had to sit with it. In March, just as Covid was shutting everything down, we had to sit with the story of Breonna Taylor, a twenty-six-year-old emergency room technician who was shot several times in her own home by Louisville, Kentucky, police with a no-knock warrant. In May, the world had to sit with the horrific footage of the murders of two men: Ahmaud Arbery, who was cornered by three white men in Georgia, and then shot because he was jogging in their neighborhood while Black, and George Floyd as he lay dying facedown on the concrete, hands cuffed behind his back while a dead-eyed cop pressed his knee on his neck for at least eight minutes and forty six seconds. Two other cops held down the 6'4", 223-pound Floyd, while a fourth held back a screaming crowd. Floyd pleaded "I can't breathe!" repeatedly, even called out for his mama, and still the demons did not move.

It's an American shame that racism doesn't rest, even in a damn pandemic. Suddenly, perhaps one could say *finally*, all over the world there is the heavy footfall of protesters in the name of Black lives. Here in Atlanta, Rayshard Brooks is killed by police in June, adding fuel to the fire, and a Wendy's goes up in flames. Helicopters circle the city like buzzards, ambulances blare in the distance, and every day at 7 p.m., residents stop whatever it is they are doing to step out of their homes or go to their windows to clap for frontline workers. Even though the optics of the marches are hopeful and make me feel like maybe, just maybe, a change gon' come, I still ask my husband not to walk the dog too late. I bargain with ancestors known and unknown to protect my family. And I get comfortable with the weight of a 9 mm in my hand.

This is why a couple of times a week I put down my phone, close my computer, wrestle the iPad away from my kid, check my purse for wallet, keys, masks, and sanitizer, jump in the car, and *go*.

"Look baby!"

Colors kaleidoscope by as our car creeps through the dark of Krog Street Tunnel. Artists with graffiti dreams come here and put up their work: ornate murals and proud, ordinary tags.

"Ooooo Mommy," my daughter whispers. "It's like an outside museum!" The cupcakes sit pretty in the passenger seat, and I'm feeling adventurous, having turned off the GPS and making my way to the beauty supply. Even though it's been almost four years since our family moved here, I'm still unfamiliar with much of the city's streets. Our car creeps toward the lip of the tunnel; to our right, a group of young Black children and adults dressed in black T-shirts and blue jeans stand in front of a tripod camera. The kids look to be only a year or two older than my daughter, who hasn't seen her friends in more than two months. She watches them closely, offers a brief wave and a shy, "Hi."

I am not so demure. "Beautiful!" I shout, clapping. "Looking good y'all!"

The adults smile; the children stare back at me curiously. I peep my enthusiasm and I am not ashamed. How can I not speak beauty into these children, even for ten seconds at a street light? With each sonic clap of my hands, I mean to loose any less-than, White lie that might be hardening in their minds—or spines. Both love and rage fuel my fervor. And my patience with the unreasonable attention Whiteness demands is thin as gossamer silk.

The light turns green and we carry on. "Siri, play 'Invincible,'" I say, another *Spider-Verse* banger, and I watch my kid through the rearview mirror, bopping her head like a '90s hip-hop head and singing the chorus:

> *I gotta stop feeling invisible*
> *And start feeling invincible*

She gazes out the window with a seriousness beyond her years and…oh, my heart. Her father and I have not yet discussed the murders with her, nor have we had the requisite

"What it means to be Black in America" talk, though I suspect she's paying attention. I just haven't wanted to lay that particular burden on her lap. Hell, she's still trying to wrap her head around why she can't see or hug her friends, why she has to wear a mask everywhere. Once a week, without fail, she announces loudly, with crossed arms and a no-nonsense stomp, "I hate the corona!"

Time is running out, I know. Babygirl will be in kindergarten soon, and we will have less control over the information that comes her way, perhaps as it should be. For now, we are protecting what my nephew Justin calls "Black innocence," that precious, fairy-dusted time when her voice is still teeny and Daddy is *actually* magic, and when she snuggles in bed with me, she asks, "Hold hands?" We're telling her, "Black is beautiful." We're framing her art and putting it on the wall. We're telling her "You got this!" And "We are so proud of you!" And "We love you." And "We are here."

Even these joyrides have become intentional, teachable moments. Church, if you've got ears to hear. I'm playing Minnie Riperton's "Les Fleurs"; "Blackbird" by The Beatles *and* the Dionne Farris version; Earth, Wind & Fire's "Shining Star"; Beyoncé's "Brown Skin Girl"; OutKast's "So Fresh, So Clean." When my daughter's lids get heavy, I put on Alice Coltrane's "Journey in Satchidananda" like a lullaby. Sharing this music—this medicine—with her mends me. I watch closely as she takes in song, and I am thrilled when she says, "Again!" I mean to impress her, blaze new pathways in her brain, open up portals, blow her mind. Because to me, these ain't just joyrides. They freedom rides too.

A protest march heads south up Argonne Avenue toward Central Park and halts traffic like a railroad stop. This particular procession is a motley crew of walkers, roller skaters, skate-boarders, and cars; small enough not to overwhelm this residential street, but large enough to summon the police helicopter hovering overhead. In the number, a gray Cutlass creeps by like a parade float blasting N.W.A.'s "Fuck Tha Police," Ice Cube testifying, *A young nigga got it bad 'cause I'm brown.*

The audacity, yo—of the driver, of Cube, who master-minded this middle finger to the LAPD. It's been thirty-three years since this track dropped, and I'm still both galvanized and gagged every time I hear it. Galvanized because "FTP" so deftly captures the fury young Black people feel when we hear the news that yet another police officer paid to protect and serve our community has, instead, murdered one of us. Gagged because such a song exists. Endures.

The car drives by with the booming system, and, without thinking, I shift into park, put on my mask, and tell babygirl "Don't move." Then I step outside and pump my fist in the air.

The beat still goes hard.

Empty streets during Atlanta's infamous rush hour feel apocalyptic, but I won't complain. There are still things to celebrate. Tomorrow my husband and I will wake up early and decorate the outside of the car with streamers and balloons and affix a poster board to the door that says HAPPY GRADUA-TION MIA PEARL! We will drive the not quite mile to her school and line up behind the other cars. Teachers and staff will stand side by side in the parking lot, masked up and wearing matching blue and white T-shirts that say GRADUATING CLASS 2020. DRIVE-THRU EDITION. When the parade begins, these women and men who have watched over our babies, some of them for years, will clap, cheer, and wipe away tears while songs like "Can't Stop the Feeling!" blare through portable speakers.

Parents will drive slowly through the parking lot while the children stay in their respective vehicles; some belted into their booster seats, others in the front seat or hoisted through the sunroof—everyone in the car wearing a mask. Some will wave, while others will appear stoic, maybe stunned that this is the graduation they've waited all year for. Nevertheless, they will accept their diplomas, gift bags, and a cupcake and drive off into a new reality.

Today, however, there's nothing left to do but go home, maybe put a steak on the grill, make a salad and have dinner on the porch, amen. As we turn right on Ponce, I decide there's time for one more jam. I pick up my phone, push the side button, and say: "Siri, play 'Whip My Hair,' by Willow."

"YES," Babygirl says from the backseat, like she won a bet. This song is one of our anthems, all urgency and light, and I crank the volume loud enough so that the bass seeps into our skin like Reiki. Willow Smith begins her chant, and my girl tosses her beloved leaf dramatically to the other side of the car.

> *Hop up out the bed, turn my swag on*
> *Pay no attention to them haters because we whip 'em off...*

Lil mama is in her own video. Perched on the edge of her booster seat, she is shimmying her shoulders, performing like she's on an episode of RuPaul's *Drag Race*, lip-synching for her life. She's giving *me* life.

"YASSSSSSS," I holler, her noble hype man from the driver's seat. "I SEE YOU DAUGHTER!!!"

At this big up, her focus deepens and she dances even harder. I grip the steering wheel and rock right along with her, whipping my teeny weeny 'fro like it's forty-eight-inch remy, honey.

Right now, nothing else matters.

"Louder, Mommy!"

She knows all the words and I do too. I turn to her in the backseat and sing, *So what's up?*

Babygirl picks up on the call-and-response: *Yeaaaahhhhhh.*

Then, together, we do what the song says: We turn our backs. We whip our hair. We shake 'em off.

How to Make a Tea Cake

L. Lamar Wilson

for Annie Pearl Long, Glenis Redmond, & so many

Sweep the hate the day gave you out the door first,
Then let Dawn-dewed hands spoon into a warm pan

Enough butter & shortening to thicken the flour
That always does the trick. Think of all the children

Whose laughter soon will fill the empty spaces he &
He & she left, how sweet their unhinged bliss. Taste

& seethe browned sugar & an egg you've whisked,
See how they dimple the dough—not unlike

The dimples the sight of such simple wonder incites
In your own kissed mien—how vanilla, lemon,

Buttermilk & baking soda take the heat off
The salt & nutmeg. Feel the leavening happen

As your pointer presses pecans inside, kept whole
Because this bread can hold them. They'll hide

In plain sight like a lover's gaze. Kneading
The dough, etch a scroll into the pulp at the center,

&, without anyone spying, lift pink heels, just so,
As the stove door seals the deals you've made

With the Ones with So Many Names to fix it
Like They promised. Now watch this meal

The day beat into bland & panned, rise, settle
& quicken from its sarcophagus, vamp the hiss-

Moan you hum until your *pièce de résistance* perfumes
The entire room, until ah, you know it's ready

To come out, join you, seated atop the range, its heat
Rousing your undulating waist, your bottom

Lip aquiver, whetted. Take all the time you need here. Part
The layers you smooth with tips of fingers wet with ginger,

Slick with salt. Then, slip a sliver into your own mouth.
Savor your hand-made savior. I think of you now,

Feasting then as if you knew we—your brothers
& sisters, your children becoming others'

Lovers, fathers, & mothers each day, coming &
Going so fast we could not see you fighting this hunger

Eating away inside every day—would always need
So much, always take what you give so freely

To yourself when we aren't looking. O how does a man,
Born of a woman, know so little of how joy tastes!

Burden Hill Apothecary & Babalú-Ayé Prepare Stinging Nettle Tea

We don't die. We be fruitful & multiply like
The Good Master say. Fields of okra, snap peas,
Collards, cabbage spring out the ground, so many
Bullets sagging on the vine, you can hear 'em holla
Pull me. Cut me. Watch me grin. We oblige. So much
Green 'tween our waists & toes, we can't see
The clay caked in the spurs cutting our heels
For the pines that shade us. We tramp
Them cones they shed that seed the soil
That keeps us alive, our loins spilling,
More mouths begging to be filled
Every day. Dem peckerwoods would turn
Every limb into a grave, if Our Maker let 'em.
You talk 'bout how they strung up Claude,
But you done forgot that high yella sot Cellos.
Smashed his skull twain under that magnolia
Over yonder, where he seasoned these here roots
I'll boil to break that fever you so 'fraid
Won't loose you, but every season, more squash,
Kale, peanuts, melon split open, so sweet, so sweet,
Every body beg to sink they teeth in deep. Like
Them weeds we yank from this here earth,
We won't die. We your worst nightmare.
Shoot one of us down, & our chirren's chirren's
Seeds'll take root & shoot up right here like

Our pappy's pappy's done. Mustards, limas,
Sweet potatoes, whites too. Our roots too deep.
You can't kill us all. Think of all that cane
You so keen to suck on. Drag that stalk
Too long, that juice'll turn bitter as the laughter
In your throat & choke. Don't let them fool you
Into cuttin' your tongues out your own
Mouths. These here are the best of times, where
The sun don't stop shinin' till you can smell
The moonshine midnight riders crawlin'
Out they bed to climb in yours & rub
'Gainst you till you sang like locusts
In heat, a low hum, a steady moan, till they
Kingdom come & morning light appear.

Before Claude Neal could face trial for the accused murder of Lola Cannady, a white childhood playmate and presumed lover, a lynch mob killed and dismembered him on October 26, 1934, outside Marianna, Florida, exhibiting and distributing his body parts among the several thousand who had traveled from far and wide to witness the spectacle. On June 16, 1943, after Cellos Harrison won a two-year battle to overturn a murder conviction with a state Supreme Court ruling, another lynch mob took him outside town and murdered him as well. Burden Hill is one of this rural North Florida town's oldest Black communities, and this speaker is the persona of an ancestor who survived these traumas.

The Purpose of a House

Emily Bernard

My friend Maurice Berger, a writer, art curator, and social-justice advocate, died in the first stages of the pandemic, just as stay-at-home orders spread, like the virus itself, throughout the United States. I was already in an active struggle—not quite a losing battle but certainly not a winning one—with fear and anxiety. Maurice's death knocked me over. I took to the darkness, like a drug, sleeping with the shades drawn. "I have no fight in me," I told my husband when I was awake and upright, scaring him half to death.

One morning, when I was trying to summon the will to rise and meet the day in some fashion, I was, simultaneously, working on an image that had been tugging at me. Early in the Covid-19 crisis, I had started composing an essay that I intended as a sort of homage to nonessential touching. I was in the flow before Maurice died, and phrases and even sentences were coming and fitting together in one of those rare, prime moments when everything works.

Something led me back to an image that morning, as I lay on my side, facing the wall. I was remembering a moment from the before, a mundane encounter with a barista at my favorite coffee shop, thinking of its value, unappreciated by me at the time. I was remembering receiving a cup of coffee from this stranger, a tattooed, sprightly, dark-haired, bespectacled young white woman. It was an unseasonably warm March day, and the young woman and I seemed to be volleying good cheer back and forth, just because we felt like it. Our fingers touched as she presented me with my coffee. They touched again when we traded cash for coins (how dirty money is, another new awareness). In that moment with the barista, I thought about the pleasure I received every Sunday during the Eucharist, looking into the eyes of the chalice bearer, usually a friend, reciting the traditional phrases we were both taught long ago to exchange at that sacred moment. I wanted to capture what both of those moments felt like, back in the before. Polite and intimate, I thought. Safe. *Legal, tender.*

The phrase rumbled through me steadily, gaining force, suffusing me with light. Legal, tender. Maybe this was Maurice reaching me, telling me to get up and write. And I did get up, arrived at my big wooden desk, and sat down to set out and see how far that phrase would take me.

Ahmaud Arbery was gunned down on February 23. Maurice died one month later.

I didn't know about Arbery's death until May, when most of the world was treated to the video of his murder. I was working. But Ahmaud Arbery was dead. I was aware of it in the manner, I believe, that most Black people who live in this country are aware of such events. I make mental notes—which state? which town? which road? which corner?—gleaning all of this information while knowing that nowhere, really, is safe. Danger can spring at any moment.

Generations of Black writers have described this experience. W. E. B. Du Bois called it double consciousness, the psychological dissonance caused by living both Black and human in the world. Perhaps we are only beginning to understand the cost of living with such a soundtrack in the back of your mind, the refrain of Black death.

I was trying to keep everything under control inside the walls that surround me.

When my twin daughters' school went remote, there was some relief in having them at home all the time. They are fourteen, recent graduates of eighth grade. Born in Ethiopia, they became U.S. citizens when we adopted them as infants. Middle school was difficult for both of my girls. Let's just say that they have emerged from these years with a keen appreciation of the way that racism works in subtle (and not so subtle) ways in liberal communities.

Over the past three years, I became one of *those* parents. I had the time and the resources, the autonomy at my job, to meet with teachers and administrators when my daughters and I agreed that such meetings were necessary. My background, as an academic and a child of professionals, makes me bold when it comes to most encounters with authority figures, particularly at school, so I was not intimidated when I had to intervene on my children's behalf on several occasions. This was something my mother had to do for me and my brothers, for some of the same reasons, forty years ago, in the slowly desegregating South. I shook my head grimly when I noted the enduring similarities between our experiences, but we soldiered on, as Black people do, and I was glad for the lessons in perseverance and valuing yourself no matter what others (white people) thought—lessons that my mother gave me that I could now pass on to my children.

I could see a noticeable difference in my daughters' demeanor after the first couple of weeks at home. I read an article about how other Black children were thriving in remote learning, not having to deal with the race-related struggles that they endured in school. I thought this applied to my girls. So there was some sort of silver lining, after all.

"The purpose of a house is to keep the outside world out," our contractor told us when we moved into our home three years ago. If it weren't for the need to walk my dog, I would spend most of every day inside, not only because of the lockdown. Three years in, and I am still constantly aware of my dark skin in this affluent, predominantly white neighborhood, even though most of my neighbors have been nothing but outwardly welcoming to me and my family. When I wrote on social media about living and working as a Black person in white spaces, particularly during the lockdown and the international uprising against racism and police violence, neighbors I hardly know liked the post, expressed compassion, and pledged a new awareness.

When I walk my dog these days, I am most often alone on the roads of my neighborhood. I like it that way. I can walk without my mask, free from the fear of contagion. And I wonder about the neighbors who expressed those sentiments of welcome. From behind all of these closed doors and shut windows, can they see me now?

I was glad to be able to keep my children safe from more demoralizing experiences at school. Still, memories crept in. It was as if, not having to deal with it in the day-to-day, my daughters were suddenly free to experience their wounds in a deep way for the first time. Three years of being one of very few

Black children in her classrooms had left Isabella feeling both hyper-visible and invisible, a jarring and alienating experience many Black people know well. Now that she was at home with her parents, she told me, even her guidance counselor's good wishes felt like an intrusion. I asked Isabella's teachers to leave her be. For Giulia, I arranged a restorative-justice session with a teacher who, after some education, had acknowledged the ways in which he had harmed her. When students made fun of her hair, he blamed her. When a group of boys mocked her for wearing a T-shirt that read "The Future is Female," she felt that her teacher did not effectively stand up for her. Giulia had thrived in spite of him, emerging as a leader and guiding discussions in his classroom about racism and sexism.

My daughters were suffering from the echoes of their three years in middle school. Their days inside were still and peaceful; the memories were dynamic and vivid. Communication as a road to healing was something that I believed in—something I knew I needed to model if I wanted them to believe in it too. Human connection. Making meaning out of suffering. Breaking down barriers and insisting on a common humanity through truth-telling.

And then George Floyd died, and the world was, once again, invited to watch the destruction of a Black human being. The video was made by a courageous teenage Black girl. It was a triumphant, essential act, and one that will likely cost her for the rest of her life.

I knew there were videos. I was glad there were videos. I did not, and would never, watch a video of anyone's murder. We are all indebted to the courageous witnesses among us. Yet no one should have been able to watch George Floyd die, except people who loved him, and God.

To know of the murders, to know of all the murders, to know that there are more than you even know about (so many kept hidden, so many human beings disappeared), to feel them, to let them in. And then the need to protect my children, not only for their sake but for the sake of their family in Ethiopia, who entrusted them to us. To keep the badness of the outside world out, and cultivate goodness inside these walls, decorated with a gallery of images meant to uphold and reinforce our family bond. To teach my girls compassion. To model for my community, to represent my people, to honor my ancestors. The prongs of faith and duty: two sides of a bridle.

One of my oldest friends called me just before a scheduled phone meeting. The screen lit up with her name—not her given name, but one of my pet names for her. I pressed a button, and we were suddenly face-to-face, though hundreds of miles apart. We looked at each other and sighed at the world. We are more than thirty-five years into an intimate relationship that is rich with all kinds of shorthand. She mentioned having watched a video. "Not the murder video," I said, referring to footage of the death of George Floyd. We're close enough; she knew what I meant. I was shuffling the notes I needed for the meeting, my eyes diverted from the screen.

She was still, frozen not by a glitch but by a truth she knew I didn't want to hear. I could feel it. I stopped shuffling and looked up. "Yes," she said. She is white.

A current of panic, dread, and anguish flamed up my arm and into the hand that was holding my phone.

"How could you?"

I thought of the girl who took the video. I thought of my girls and all I was trying to protect them from.

"I think I just needed…to see," she said.

"No," I said, alarmed by the note of terror in my own voice.

"No," I told my daughters. "You may not watch those videos. It's not good for your soul."

I shook my finger at their teenage faces, in a clichéd gesture of top-down parenting that would otherwise count as a joke among us. They agreed. Still, it wasn't purely an act of defiance that my daughter Isabella eventually watched both videos when they appeared on her social-media feed. I asked her what it felt like to watch the men die. The George Floyd video saddened her. "I thought of Nonni," she said, referring to her Italian grandmother. "When she died, she was surrounded by people who loved her. George Floyd had no one." It was like, if she didn't watch it, she would be letting him die alone all over again, she said.

The Ahmaud Arbery video terrified her. When she cried, her body shook.

"I don't like to be touched," Isabella likes to remind me. Not wanting to be touched by her mother is an essential part of the teenage persona I have been watching her shape over the past couple of years. Textbook. It amuses me and it pains me. I miss her body. But I knew trying to hug her in that moment would only make it worse.

I watched her shoulders shudder and terror travel though her narrow frame like electricity. I stood there, less than ten feet away, my hands clasped in front of me.

He wanted his mother.

We held the restorative-justice session for Giulia over Zoom. She cried several times during the session, confessing her feelings to her teacher, who had allowed her to be teased and harangued in moments he now describes as racist and misogynistic. He confessed his ignorance and apologized sincerely for the harm he caused. I could see, even through a screen, how my daughter's pain entered him, corrected him, educated him. This happened because he let it be so. But as small as he must have felt during the session, he still had all the power. He had to show up for Giulia to heal. And show up he did.

The first time my daughter broke down, I reached out my hand to stroke her arm. We were sitting side by side at my desk, our shoulders less than five inches apart. She shrugged me off harshly. "I'm sorry for babying you," I wrote her on a piece of paper. She dropped her eyes momentarily from the screen to read it. "It's O.K.," she wrote back.

For the rest of the session, I visualized sitting on my hands while Giulia cried and cried, and her teacher watched her, tears in his own eyes. She put her head down and sobbed; while her head was down, her teacher quickly and discreetly wiped away his tears. I was touched by his determination not to make a show of his sadness. Everyone in that space, real and virtual, tiny and vast, our trinity, united through Giulia's misery, was broken, then restored, then broken again.

My daughter lifted her head and powered on, describing episodes that took place in his classroom, a testimony that hurt her all over again. She chose to speak instead of being silent.

We are inside, all of us: my husband, daughters, and me. We are a team, twenty-four seven. Ride or die. We are bound, not by blood, or even a common last name, racial identity, or country of origin. We are connected through idiom, humor, and sensibility. By our beloved dog, who gets us out into the world and then brings us back inside. By food. By talk: inside jokes, running debates, and a shared pleasure in language itself.

My daughters are growing like hothouse flowers. They stare at their bodies in the mirror. They touch their faces, indoors, in our home, which I am constantly trying to disinfect. I steal glances at them as they watch themselves in the mirror in my bedroom. I sit perfectly still on the bed, quieted by admiration and longing. I know that if I say anything I will break the spell, our silent agreement. They need to be near me; they need to act as if they don't want anything to do with me. "Our daughters have been practicing social distancing with us for a while," my husband and I joke.

I miss them. They are rarely more than twenty feet away. When I move to a different floor in our house, they often move to the same floor, in a different room, out of sight.

There were long moments in the conversation between Giulia and her teacher when she couldn't look at him. She could only look at me, her mother, whose touch she rebuffs. But I knew I was feeding her, that she was looking to me for some kind of nourishment, that I must keep my face still and open, be her mirror, her port, her light. I knew this in my bones, throughout my body. I kept my hands to myself and fed her. My husband, who is white, was at home, present as always, but I felt this was a Black mother's fight.

"It's not fair," Giulia said, staring at me.

"It's not fair," I repeated, holding her gaze.

It was only when she got what she needed from my eyes that she turned back to look her teacher in the face, their images mere inches apart.

My house is sturdy, for the most part. I dream of more renovations, of making it better, stronger, safer, and more beautiful, for my children, for my team. But I can't keep them safe. I can't keep the outside world out. All of my efforts are violated by phones and screens and the truth of Black American life itself. A few days after she told me she watched the murders, Isabella showed me a video of a Black girl with braids and deep brown skin, just like hers, telling her father that she might be killed for the color of her skin. "I'm sorry," her father says, taking her into his arms.

"See?" my daughter said. "He couldn't say no." She kept the screen facing me, daring me to contradict the girl or the father.

"Yes," I said.

All I could think was, Lucky father. At least his daughter lets him hold her.

"How did I do, Mommy?" Giulia asked quietly after the session with her teacher.

"You did great," I told her.

"What did I do?" So quietly, she breathed the words more than spoke them.

"You told the truth. You didn't lie. You didn't pretend those experiences didn't bother you," I said. "That way? Those kinds of lies? They'll kill you."

I still want to write an essay about intimacy, a stranger's touch. A quiet celebration of life, not death, not yet. A story about meaningful human transactions, absent of violence, brimming only with love. Love of self, of other, of life. Legal, tender.

Lockdown Prayer

Honorée Fanonne Jeffers

> *Yahweh est mon pasteur; je ne manquerai de rien.*
> Psalm 23:1 (en Français)

> *Yalla moy burr.*
> Wolof proverb

For these clean nails
For these rolls of living fat
these too-useful hands   impatient feet

> *[if i learned this psalm in french*
> *the Lord would listen to me]*

For this heart pounding
disobedient chants
this spirit   witnessing
white men build new ships
this mouth whispering cantos
this roof   this bed   this water
     Even water
a past enemy   now comrade
now enemy again

> *[if i wrapped myself in this*
> *caped myth of undying Black*
> *women   this miracle*
> *of clicking hoodoo]*

For this food and a mother's
prayer   *yea   for the nourishment*
of our fragile bodies   yea   for the survival
of navel string faith
For this coping   this air
pushing through vents
this car sitting outside   a reminder
I can't go anywhere

> *[if i believed until He built a rock]*

For this phone that buzzes
For the dead who touch
in dreams   these African
syllables of mourning
          Yalla moy burr   God is king
God is master with no whip
mercy after no touch   no noise
in a locked-down village

> *[if i reached back*
>   *to grab the slippery*
>   *hand of God   i would give*
>   *praise   i would free myself]*

For this day   this breath

> *[if i breathed]*

for Valerie

Out There, Nobody Can Hear You Scream

Latria Graham

In the spring of 2019, right before I leave for my writing residency in Great Smoky Mountains National Park, my mama tries to give me a gun. A Ruger P89DC that used to belong to my daddy, it's one of the few things she kept after his death. Even though she doesn't know how to use it, she knows that I do. She's just had back surgery, and she's in no shape to come and get me if something goes wrong up in those mountains, so she tries to give me this. I turn the gun over in my hand. It's a little dusty and sorely out of use. The metal sends a chill up my arm.

Even though it is legal for me to have a gun, I cannot tell if, as a Black woman, I'd be safer with or without it. Back in 2016, I watched the aftermath of Philando Castile's killing as it was streamed on Facebook Live by his girlfriend, Diamond Reynolds. Castile was shot five times at close range by a police officer during a routine traffic stop, when he went to reach for his license, registration, and permit to carry a gun. His girlfriend's four-year-old daughter watched him dying from the back seat. In his case, having the proper paperwork didn't matter.

I'll be in the Smokies for six weeks in early spring, the park's quiet season, staying in a cabin on my own. My local contact list will be short: the other writer who had been awarded the residency, our mentor, maybe a couple of park employees. If something happens to me, there will likely be no witnesses, no one to stream my last moments. When my mother isn't looking, I make sure the safety is on, and then I put the gun back where she got it. I leave my fate to the universe.

Before I back out of our driveway, my mama insists on saying a protective blessing over me. She has probably said some version of this prayer over my body as long as I've been able to explore on my own.

In 2018, I wrote an article for *Outside* magazine titled "We're Here. You Just Don't See Us," about my family's relationship to nature and the stereotypes and obstacles to access that Black people face in the outdoors. As a journalist, that piece opened doors for me, like the residency in Great Smoky Mountains National Park.

It also inspired people to write me.

Two years later, the messages still find me on almost every social media platform: Twitter, Instagram, even LinkedIn. They come through my Gmail. Most of them sound the same—they thank me for writing the article and tell me how much it meant to them to see a facet of the Black experience represented in a major outdoor magazine. They express apprehension about venturing into new places and ask for my advice on recreating outside of their perceived safety zone.

They ask what they can do to protect themselves in case they wind up in a hostile environment.

Folks have their desires and dreams tied up in the sentences they send me. They want to make room for the hope that I cautiously decided to write about in 2018.

Back then, as a realist, I didn't want my essay's ending to sound too optimistic. But I still strayed from talking about individual discrimination in the parks, often perpetrated by white visitors, like the woman who recently told an Asian American family that they "can't be in this country" as they finished their hike near Mount Tamalpais in Marin County, California, this past Fourth of July. Or the now famous "BBQ Becky" who called the police on two Black men at Lake Merritt in Oakland, California, in 2018, for using a charcoal grill in a non-charcoal-grill-designated area. Nor did I mention that when I venture into new spaces, I am always doing the math: noting the lengths of dirt roads so I know how far I have to run if I need help, taking stock of my gas gauge to ensure I have enough to get away.

I have been the target of death threats since 2015, when I started writing about race. I wasn't sure if magazine readers were ready for that level of candid conversation, so in 2018 I left that tidbit out.

There are risks to being Black in the outdoors; I am simply willing to assume them. And that's why I struggle to answer the senders of these messages, because I don't have any tips to protect them. Instead I invoke magical thinking, pretending that if I don't hit the reply button, the communication didn't happen. Sometimes technology helps: when I let the message requests sit unaccepted in Instagram, the app deletes them after four weeks.

I deem myself a coward. I know I am a coward.

There are two messages that still haunt me.

The first is an email from a woman who wanted to know what she and her brown-skinned husband should do if they encounter another campground with a Confederate flag hanging in the check-in office. She described to me a night of unease, of worrying if they and their daughter would be safe. I filed her email so deep in my folders that I don't even think I can find it anymore. I was dying to forget that I had no salve for her suffering.

The second was even more personal. It came via Facebook Messenger, from a woman named Tish. In it she says: "I came across a read of yours when I was searching African Americans and camping. I want to rent an RV and go with my family. I live in Anderson, South Carolina. Had a daughter that also attended SCGSAH. Is there a campground you recommend that is not too far and yes where I would feel comfortable? Thank you."

The signaling in it, of tying me to her daughter, examining my background enough to offhandedly reference the South Carolina arts high school I attended and saying, *Please, my daughter is similar to you.*

I leave her message in the unread folder.

These women have families, and they too are trying to pray a blessing over the ones they love while leaving room for them to play, grow, and learn—the same things their white peers want for their offspring. In their letters, they hang some of their hopes for a better America on me, on any advice I might be able to share.

I haven't written back because I haven't had any good advice to offer, and that is what troubles me. These letters have been a sore spot, festering, unwilling to heal.

Now, in the summer of 2020, there are bodies hanging from trees again, and that has motivated me to pick up my pen. Our country is trying to figure out what to do about racial injustice and systemic brutality against Black people. It's time to tell those who wrote to me what I know.

Dear Tish, Alex, Susan, and everyone else:

I want to apologize for the delayed reply. It took a long time to gather my thoughts. When I wrote that article back in 2018, I was light on the risks and violence and heavy-handed on hope. I come to you now as a woman who insists we must be heavy-handed on both if we are to survive.

I write to you in the middle of the night, with the only light on the entire street emanating from my headlamp. Here in upstate South Carolina, we are in the midst of a regional blackout. My time outdoors has taught me how to sit with the darkness—how to be equipped for it. Over the years, I have found ways to work within it, or perhaps in spite of it. If there's anything I can do, maybe it's help you become more comfortable with the darkness too.

But before I tell you any more, I want you to understand that you and I are more than our pain. We are more than the human-rights moment we are fighting for.

It isn't an exaggeration to say that the *Outside* article changed my life. People paid me for speaking gigs and writing workshops. They put me on planes and flew me across the country to talk about equity, inclusion, and accountability. I know the statistics, the history, the arguments that organizations give about why they have no need to change. I call them on it.

I have to apologize for not being prepared for the heaviness of this mantle at the time. I have to admit my hesitation back then to call white supremacy and racism by their names. The unraveling of this country in the summer of 2020 forced me to reckon with my actions, my place in the natural world, and the fact that as a Black woman writer in America, I am tasked with telling you a terrible truth: I am so sorry. I have nothing of merit to offer you as protection.

I am reluctant to inform you that while I can challenge white people to make the outdoors a nonhostile, equitable space where you can be your authentic selves, when the violence of white supremacy turns its eyes toward you, there's nothing I can give you to protect yourself from its gaze and dehumanization.

I do not wish to ask you to have to be brave in the face of inequality. This nation's diminished moral capacity for seeing Black people as human beings is not our fault. Their perception of you isn't your problem—it's theirs, the direct result of the manifest-destiny and "anybody can become anything in America" narratives they have bought into. We are made to suffer so they can slake their guilt. I want you to be unapologetically yourselves.

I check with my fellow Black outdoor friends, and they say they've gotten your email and messages, too. They also waffle on what to say, telling y'all to carry pepper spray or dress in a nonthreatening way. I am troubled about instructing people who have already been socially policed to death—to literal, functional death—to change the way they walk, talk, dress, or take up space in order to seem less threatening to those who are uncomfortable with seeing our brown skin.

I have no talisman that can shield you from the white imagination. The incantation "I'm calling the police" will be less potent coming from your mouth and will not work in the same way. In the end, your utterance could backfire, causing you more pain.

I want to tell you to make sure you know wilderness first aid, to carry the ten essentials, to practice Leave No Trace, so no one has any right to bother you as you enjoy your day. I want to tell you to make sure you know what it means not to need, to be so prepared that you never have to ask for a shred, scrap, or ribbon of compassion from anybody.

But that is misanthropic—maybe, at its core, inhumane.

I resist the urge to pass on to you the instinct my Black foremothers ingrained in me to make ourselves small before the denizens of this land. I have watched this scenario play out since I was a child: my father, a tall fifty-year-old man with big hands, being called "boy" by some white person and playing along, willing to let them believe that they have more power than he does, even though I have watched him pin down a 400-pound hog on his own. I have seen my mother shrink behind her steering wheel, pulled over for going five miles above the speed limit on her way to her mom's house. She taught me and my brother the rules early: only speak when spoken to, do not ask questions, do not make eye contact, do not get out of the car, keep your hands on the wheel, comply, comply, comply, even if it costs you your agency. Never, ever show your fear. Cry in the driveway when you get to your destination alive. Those traffic stops could've ended very differently. The corpses of Samuel DuBose, Maurice Gordon, Walter Scott, and Rayshard Brooks prove that.

I will not pass on these generational curses; they were ways of compensating for anti-Black thinking. They should never have been your burden.

It would be easy to tell you to always be aware of your surroundings, to never let your guard down, to be prepared to record in case you run into an Amy Cooper or if a white man points an AR15 at you and your friends as you take a break from riding your motorcycles, hoping to make the most of a sunny almost-summer day in Virginia.

These moments—tied to a phone, always tensed in fear—are not what time in nature is supposed to be. Yet the videos seem to be the only way America at large believes us. It took an eight-minute-and-forty-six-second snuff film for the masses to wake up and challenge the unjust system our people have had to navigate for more than 400 years. They are killing us for mundane things—running, like Ahmaud Arbery; playing in the park, like Tamir Rice. They've always killed us for unexceptional reasons. But now the entire country gets to watch life leak away from Black bodies in high definition.

I started writing this on the eve of what should have been Breonna Taylor's twenty-seventh birthday. The police broke into her home while she was sleeping and killed her. I write to you during a global pandemic, during a time when Covid-19 has had a disproportionate impact on Black and brown communities. I conclude my thoughts during what should have been the summer before Tamir Rice's senior year of high school. All the old protective mechanisms and safety nets Black people created for ourselves aren't working anymore. Sometimes compliance is not enough. Sometimes they kill you anyway.

Having grown up in the Deep South, I have long been aware of the threat of racial violence, of its symbolism. In middle school, many of my peers wore the Dixie Outfitters T-shirts that were in vogue in that part of the country during the late nineties. The shirts often featured collages of the Confederate flag, puppies, and shotguns on the front, with slogans like "Stand and Fight for Southern Rights" and "Preserving Southern Heritage Since 1861" printed on the back.

I was eleven years old, and these kids—and their commitment to a symbol from a long-lost war—signaled that they believed I shouldn't be in the same classroom with them, that I didn't belong in their world.

But that was nothing compared with the routine brutality perpetrated upon Black people in my home state. In 2010, years before the deaths of Trayvon Martin, Michael Brown, and Sandra Bland, there was the killing of Anthony Hill. Gregory Collins, a white worker at a local poultry plant not far from my family farm, shot and killed Hill, his Black coworker. He dragged Hill's body behind his pickup truck for ten miles along the highways near my grandmother's house, leaving a trail of blood and tendons. Abandoned on the road, the corpse was found with a single gunshot wound to the head and a rope tied around what remained of the body. Collins was sentenced for manslaughter. Five years ago, a radicalized white supremacist murdered nine Black parishioners as they prayed in Mother Emanuel African Methodist Episcopal Church in Charleston. South Carolina is one of two states that still does not have a hate-crime law.

Before my writing residency, I did not own a range map. Traditionally, these are used to depict plant and animal habitats and indicate where certain species thrive. Ranges are often defined by climate, food sources, water availability, the presence of predators, and a species's ability to adapt.

My friend J. Drew Lanham taught me I could apply this sort of logic to myself. A Black ornithologist and professor of wildlife ecology, he was unfazed by what happened to birdwatcher Christian Cooper in Central Park—he's had his own encounters with white people who can't understand why he might be standing in a field with binoculars in his hand. Several years ago he wrote a piece for *Orion* magazine called "Nine Rules for the Black Birdwatcher."

"Carry your binoculars—and three forms of identification—at all times," he wrote. "You'll need the binoculars to pick that tufted duck out of the flock of scaup and ring-necks. You'll need the photo ID to convince the cops, FBI, Homeland Security, and the flashlight-toting security guard that you're not a terrorist or escaped convict." Drew frequently checks the Southern Poverty Law Center's hate-group map and the Equal Justice Initiative's "Lynching in America" map and overlays them. The blank spaces are those he might travel to.

I never thought to lay out the data like that until the day I went to Abrams Creek.

Three weeks into my residency, I made an early-afternoon visit to the national-park archives. I needed to know what information they had on Black people. I left with one sheet of paper—a slave schedule that listed the age, sex, and race ("black" or "mulatto") of bodies held in captivity. There were no names. There were no pictures. I remember chiding myself for believing there might be.

Emotionally wrought and with a couple of hours of sunlight ahead of me, I decided to go for a drive to clear my mind. I came to the Smokies with dreams of writing about the natural world. I wanted to talk about the enigmatic Walker sisters, the park's brook trout restoration efforts, and the ground-breaking agreement that the National Park Service reached with the Eastern Band of Cherokee Indians about their right to sustainably harvest the edible sochan plant on their ancestral lands. My Blackness, and curiosity about the Black people living in this region, was not at the front of my mind. I naively figured I would learn about them in the historical panels of the visitor's center, along with the former white inhabitants and the Cherokee. I thought there would be a book or a guide about them.

There was nothing.

Vacations are meant to be methods of escapism. Believing this idyllic wilderness to be free of struggle, of complicated emotions, allows visitors to enjoy their day hikes. Many tourists to Great Smoky Mountains National Park see what they believe it has always been: rainbow-emitting waterfalls, cathedrals of green, carpets of yellow trillium in the spring.

The majority never venture more than a couple of miles off the main road. They haven't trained their eyes to look for the overgrown homesites of the park's former inhabitants through the thick underbrush. Using the park as a side trip from the popular tourist destinations like Dollywood and Ripley's Believe It or Not, they aren't hiking the trails that pass by cemeteries where entire communities of white, enslaved, and emancipated people lived, loved, worked, died, and were buried, some, without ever being paid a living wage. Slavery here was arguably more intimate. An owner had four slaves, not 400. But it happened.

There is a revisionist fantasy that Americans cling to about the people in this region of North Carolina and Tennessee: that they were dirt-poor, struggled to survive, and wrestled the mountains into submission with their own brute strength. In reality, many families hired their sharecropping neighbors, along with Black convicts on chain gangs, to do the hard labor for them.

These corrections of history aren't conversations most people are interested in having.

After a fruitless stop at Fontana Dam, the site of a former African American settlement where I find precious little to see, I try to navigate back to where I'm staying. Cell service is spotty. My phone's GPS takes me on a new route along the edge of the park, through Happy Valley, which you can assume from the moniker is less than happy.

Early spring in the mountains is not as beautiful as you might believe. The trees are bare, and you can see the Confederate and Gadsden flags, the latter with their coiled rattlesnakes, flapping in the wind, so they do not take you by surprise. At home after home, I see flag after flag. The banners tell me that down in this valley I am on my own, as do the corpses of Jonathan A. Ferrell and Renisha McBride,

Black people who knocked on the doors of white homeowners asking for help and were shot in response.

In the middle of this drive back to the part of the park where I belong, I round a corner to see a man burning a big pile of lumber, the flames taller than my car.

I am convinced that pyrophobia is embedded in my genes. The Ku Klux Klan was notorious for cross burnings and a willingness to torch homes. The fire over my shoulder is large enough to burn up any evidence that I ever existed. There is a man standing in his yard wearing a baseball cap and holding a drink, watching me as my white rental car creeps by. I want to ask him how to get out of here. I think of my mama's frantic phone calls going straight to voice mail. I stay in the car.

Farther down the road, another man is burning a big pile of lumber. I know it's just coincidence, that these bundles of timber were stacked before I set off down this path, but the symbolism unnerves me.

I round a bend and a familiar sign appears—a national-park placard with the words ABRAMS CREEK CAMPGROUND RANGER STATION in white letters. Believing some fresh air might settle my stomach and strengthen my nerves, I decide to enter that section of the park. The road I drive is the border between someone's property and the park. Uneven, it forces me to go slowly.

The dog is at my car before I recognize what is happening. It materializes as a strawberry blond streak bumping up against my driver's side door. Tall enough to reach my face, it is gnashing at my side mirror, trying to bite my reflection.

I'm not scared of dogs, but this one, with its explicit hostility, gives me pause.

Before emancipation, dogs hunted runaway slaves by scent, often maiming the quarry to keep them in place until their owner could arrive. During the civil rights movement, dogs were weaponized by police. In the modern era, use of K-9 units to intimidate and attack is so common that police have referred to Black people as "dog biscuits."

I force myself to keep driving.

When I reach the ranger station, the building is dark: closed for the season. I see a trail inviting me to walk between two shortleaf pines, but I decline. There is something in me that is more wound up than it has a right to be. No one knows my whereabouts. Despite making up 13 percent of the population, more than 30 percent of all missing persons in the U.S. in 2019 were Black. A significant portion of these cases are never covered by the news. The chances of me disappearing without a mention are higher than I'd like.

There are three cars in the little gravel parking lot. A pair of men, both bigger than me, are illegally flying drones around the clearing, and there is palpable apprehension around my presence. They don't acknowledge me, and I can't think of what I'm supposed to say to convince them I'm not a threat. I have no idea who the third car belongs to—they are somewhere in my periphery, real and not real, an ancillary portion of my calculation.

I take photos of the clearing, including the cars, just in case I don't make it out. It is the only thing I know to do.

I run my odds. No one in an official capacity to enforce the rules, no cell service to call for help, little knowledge of the area. I leave. Later, my residency mentor gently suggests that maybe I don't visit that section of the park alone anymore.

I promise that there are parts of this park, and by extension the outdoors as a whole, that make visiting worth it. Time in nature is integral to my physical, spiritual, and mental health.

I chase the radiant moments, because as a person who struggles with chronic depression, the times I am enthusiastically happy are few and far between. Most of them happen outside.

I relish the moments right before sunrise up at Purchase Knob in the North Carolina section of the Smokies. The world is quiet, my mind is still, and the birds, chattering to one another, do not mind my presence. I believe this is what Eden must have been like. I still live for the nights where I sink into my sleeping pad while I cowboy camp, with nothing in or above my head except the stars. I believe in the healing power of hiking, the days when I am strong, capable, at home in my body.

The fear, on some level, will always exist. I say this to myself all the time: I know you're scared. Do it anyway.

Toward the end of my writing residency, the road to Clingmans Dome opens. At 6,643 feet, Clingmans is the highest point in Tennessee and in the park. About two days before I'm scheduled to leave, I go to see what this peak holds for me.

There is a paved trail leading to the observatory at the summit. It isn't long, just steep. Maybe it's the elevation; I have to do the hike twenty steps at a time, putting one foot in front of the other until I get to twenty, then starting over again. I catch my breath in ragged clips, and there are moments when I can feel my heartbeat throbbing in my fingertips. I'd planned to be at the top for sunset, but I realize the sun might be gone when I get there. I continue anyhow. I'm slow but stubborn.

If there's anything I appreciate about the crucible we're living in, it's the role of social media in creating a place for us when others won't. We're no longer waiting for outdoor companies to find the budget for diversity, equity, and inclusion initiatives. With the creation of a hashtag, a social media movement, suddenly we are hyper visible, proud, and unyielding.

As I make my way up the ramp toward its intersection with the Appalachian Trail, I think about Will Robinson (@akunahikes on Instagram), the first documented African American man to complete the triple crown of hiking: the Appalachian, Pacific Crest, and Continental Divide Trails. I understand that I'm following in Robinson's footsteps, and those of other Black explorers like writer Rahawa Haile (@rahawahaile) and long-haul hiker Daniel White (@theblackalachian)—people who passed this way while completing their AT through-hikes and whom I now call friends, thanks to the internet. I smile and think of them as the trail meets the pavement, and stop for a moment. We have all seen this junction.

Their stories, videos, and photographs tell me what they know of the world I'm still learning to navigate. They are the adventurers I've been rooting for since the very beginning, and now I know they're also rooting for me.

It's our turn to wish for good things for you.

When I get to the summit the world is tinged in blue, and with minimal cloud cover I can see the borders of seven states. There is nothing around me now but heaven. I'm grateful I didn't quit.

My daddy had a saying that I hated as a child: "The man on top of the mountain didn't fall there." It's a quote attributed to NFL coach Vince Lombardi, who during the fifties and sixties refused to give in to the racial pressures of the time and segregate his Green Bay Packers. It took me decades to understand what those two were trying to tell me, but standing at the top of Clingmans Dome, I get it. The trick is that there is no trick. You learn to eat fire by eating fire.

But none of us has to do it alone.

America is a vast place, and we often feel isolated because of its geography. But there are organizations around the country that have our backs: Black Outside, Inc., Color Outside, WeGotNext, Outdoor Afro, Black Folks Camp Too, Blackpackers, Melanin Base Camp, and others.

The honest discussions must happen now. I acknowledge that I am the descendant of enslaved people—folks who someone else kidnapped from their homeland and held captive in this one.

We were more than bodies then.

We are more than bodies now.

We have survived fierce things.

My ancestors survived genocide, the centuries-long hostage situation they were born into, and the tortures that followed when they called for freedom and equality. They witnessed murder. They endured as their wages and dreams were taken from them by systemic policies and physical force. And yet, because of their drive to survive, I am here.

I stand in the stream of a legacy started by my ancestors and populated by present-day Black trailblazers like outdoors journalist James Edward Mills, environmental-justice activist Teresa Baker, and conservationists Audrey and Frank Peterman. Remembering them—their struggles and triumphs—allows me to center myself in this scenery, as part of this landscape, and claim it as my history. This might be the closest thing to reparations that this country, founded on lofty ideals from morally bankrupt slaveholders, will ever give me.

I promised you at the beginning that I would be candid about the violence and even-keeled about the hope. I still have hope—I consider it essential for navigating these spaces, for being critical of America. I wouldn't be this way if I didn't know there was a better day coming for this country.

Even when hope doesn't reside within me—those days happen, too—I know that it is safely in the hands of fellow Black adventurers to hold until I am ready to reclaim my share of it. I pray almost unceasingly for your ability to understand how powerful you are. If you weren't, they wouldn't be trying to keep you out, to make sure they keep the beauty and understanding of this vast world to themselves. If we weren't rewriting the story about who belongs in these places, they wouldn't be so focused on silencing us with their physical intimidation and calls for murder.

The more we see, the more we document, the more we share, the better we can empower those who come after us. I've learned during all my years of historical research that even when white guilt, complacency, and intentional neglect try to erase our presence, there is always a trace. Now there are hundreds of us, if not thousands, intent on blazing a trail.

It is true: I cannot protect you. But there is one thing I can continue to do: let you know that you are not alone in doing this big, monumental thing. You deserve a life of adventure, of joy, of enlightenment. The outdoors are part of our inheritance. So I will keep writing, posting photos, and doing my own signaling. For every new place I visit, and the old ones I return to, my message to you is that you belong here, too.

Racism Is Terrible. Blackness Is Not.

Imani Perry

A lot of kind statements about Black people are coming from the pens and minds of white people now. That's a good thing. But sometimes, it is frankly hard to tell the difference between expressions of solidarity and gestures of absolution. (*See, I'm not a racist, I said you matter!*) Among the most difficult to swallow are social media posts and notes that I and others have received expressing sorrow and implying that Blackness is the most terrible of fates. Their worrisome chorus: "I cannot imagine…How do you…My heart breaks for you…I know you are hurting…You may not think you matter, but you matter to me." Let me be clear: I certainly know I matter. Racism is terrible. Blackness is not.

I cannot remember a time in my life when I wasn't earnestly happy about the fact of my Blackness. When my cousins and I were small, we would crowd in front of the mirrors in my grandmother's house, admiring our shining brown faces, the puffiness of our hair.

My elders taught me that I belonged to a tradition of resilience, of music that resonates across the globe, of spoken and written language that sings. If you've had the good fortune to experience a holiday with a large Black American family, you have witnessed the masterful art of storytelling, the vitality of our laughter, and the everyday poetry of our experience. The narrative boils down quite simply to this: "We are still here! Praise life, after everything, we are still here!" So many people taught us to be more than the hatred heaped upon us, to cultivate a deep self-regard no matter what others may think, say, or do. Many of us have absorbed that lesson and revel in it.

One of the classic texts in African American studies is Zora Neale Hurston's 1928 essay "How It Feels to Be Colored Me." Her playful yet profound articulation resonates for me now. She wrote, "I am not tragically colored. There is no great sorrow dammed up in my soul, nor lurking behind my eyes. I do not mind at all. I do not belong to the sobbing school of Negrohood who hold that nature somehow has given them a lowdown dirty deal and whose feelings are all hurt about it.... No, I do not weep at the world—I am too busy sharpening my oyster knife."

Some of her words, I must admit, are too hopeful, at least for me right now. In fact, I *do* weep at the world; I am, in a sense, part of the sobbing school; and I am skeptical that my lone oyster knife can cut any of the rot out of this nation. But, like Hurston, I refuse to see the story of who I am as a tragedy.

Joy is not found in the absence of pain and suffering. It exists through it. The scourges of racism, poverty, incarceration, medical discrimination, and so much more shape Black life. We live with the vestiges of slavery and Jim Crow, and with the new creative tides of anti-blackness directed toward us and our children. We know the wail of a dying man calling for his mama, and it echoes into the distant past and cuts into our deepest wounds. The injustice is inescapable. So yes, I want the world to recognize our suffering. But I do not want pity from a single soul. Sin and shame are found in neither my body nor my identity. Blackness is an immense and defiant joy. As the poet Sonia Sanchez wrote in a haiku about her power—and her struggles:

> come windless invader
> i am a carnival of
> stars a poem of blood.

People of all walks of life are protesting the violent deaths handed out by police officers. This is extraordinary both because the victims were Black—and when does Black death elicit such a response?—and because Americans in general have a hard time dealing with death. Think about how uncomfortable many Americans are with grief. You are supposed to meet it with a hidden shamefulness, tuck yourself away respectably for a season, and then return whole and recovered. But that is not at all how grief courses through life. It is emetic, peripatetic; it shakes you and stops you and sometimes disappears only to come barreling back to knock the wind out of you.

Black Americans right now are experiencing a collective grief, one that unfolds publicly. And we are unable to tuck it away. I do think Hurston would have to admit this too, were she around today. She wrote her essay before *Brown v. Board of Education*, the Montgomery bus boycott, the Birmingham Children's Crusade, the March on Washington, Freedom Summer, the Voting Rights Act, the Civil Rights Act of 1964, the rise of Black mayors, the first elected Black governor, the first Black president. She wrote her essay before we understood how tightly this nation would grasp onto its original sin even after legions of Black people came with razor-sharp oyster knives and hands full of pearls.

Black Americans continue to die prematurely—whether under the knee of a police officer, or struggling for breath on a respirator, or along the stretch of the Mississippi River known as Cancer Alley, or in the shadow of Superfund sites, or in one of the countless other ways we are caught in the spokes. The trauma is repetitive. We weep. But we are still, even in our most anguished seasons, not reducible to the fact of our grief. Rather, the capacity to access joy is a testament to the grace of living as a protest—described by Lorraine Hansberry, who, as one of the greatest playwrights in the history of American theater, wrote *A Raisin in the Sun*. Whenever she recounted the story of Black America in lectures or discussions, she pointed to the extraordinary achievements we attained under obscene degradation. "Isn't it rather remarkable that we can talk about a people who were publishing newspapers while they were still in slavery in 1827, you see?" she said during a speech in 1964.

Some of us who comment on racial inequality these days are averse to such accounts of Black history, thinking them romantic and not frank enough about the ravages of racism. So I hope that no one is confused by my words. American racism is unquestionably rapacious. To identify the achievement and exhilaration in Black life is not to mute or minimize racism, but to shame racism, to damn it to hell. The masters were wrong in the antebellum South, when they described the body-shaking, delighted chuckle of an enslaved person as simplemindedness. No, that laugh—like our music, like our language, like our movement—was a testimony that refused the terms of our degradation. In the footage of the protests over the past several weeks, we have seen Black people dancing, chanting, singing. Do not misunderstand. This is not an absence of grief or rage, or a distraction. It is insistence.

And so, I must turn the pitying gaze back upon any who offer it to me, because they cannot understand the spiritual majesty of joy in suffering. But my rejection of their account also comes with an invitation. If you join us, you might feel not only our pain but also the beauty of being human.

Mine

B. Brian Foster

If you only read the headline, you would barely know she was there: "Mr. and Mrs. Bruce Foster would like to announce the grand opening of FOSTER'S LAUNDRY CENTER." They put the building's name in big letters and spelled his name all the way out but couldn't manage to say hers: Minnie.

I never asked Daddy about the newspaper, but I watched his life long enough to know. He probably didn't mind which words the headline had and which it skipped. In his world, to be able to touch something was to be able to say it was yours, and if it was yours you could make it how you wanted it—the laundry center, the headline, Momma.

Momma and Daddy met in 1980, six years before they opened the laundry center. They were young. Momma was twenty-two. Daddy was twenty-nine. She was widowed, and he was divorced. Then, after a Halloween trip to a North Mississippi courthouse, they were married.

I have asked Momma more times than I can count why they chose to elope—"It was his wish"—and why they decided to do it on that day instead of any other. "It was his birthday." She could have stopped after the third word both times.

Momma and Daddy built the laundromat—and the first part of their life together—from nickels and dimes. Daddy was just like his daddy, a carpenter who drank Budweiser and "bumpy face" gin all day. Momma was like all the Black folks in Mississippi, willing to work with her hands to live. She traded factory jobs for factory jobs, then traded all of the money she made from them to help Daddy collect the quarters of Black folks whose factory jobs didn't pay enough for them to live and have things like washers and dryers at the same time.

There are four pictures of the laundry center that I know of. One shows the front of the building, the slanted roof reading FOS ER'S LAUNDRY CENTER. One shows my brother, as a toddler, standing in the parking lot. The other two photos show the laundry center when it was nothing but a concrete slab and matrix of two-by-fours. In one of those pictures, Daddy stands in the main entrance, his body somehow both muscular and indistinct, wearing only a pair of white shorts. His right hand holds his left wrist, looking. In the other of those pictures, Momma is standing in the same entranceway, almost exactly where Daddy was standing but not how. She is wearing a blue floral print dress and sandals. The weight of my unborn older brother pushes her body out and slightly to the left. Her hands cup the king studs that stretch up beside her. The sky looks dusk. The trees look country. She is looking directly into the camera.

"You can count dollars quicker than you count quarters, don't you think?" Momma had told me, more times than I can count—something a white loan officer at a local bank had said to her and Daddy after the laundry center's grand opening. The last time she told me that story, we were watching *Columbo* in a small apartment in East Memphis. It was March of 2021, a year after I had gotten sick from something that felt like the flu, except longer and with more coughing and less energy. I did not get tested then. I knew it was Covid-19. There was never a day when I believed I would die, but there were weeks of nights that I felt like it. I wanted my Momma, but not more than I wanted my Momma not to feel what I was feeling. I stayed home.

When Momma and I talked that day in Memphis a year later, so much had changed. Covid-19 had been credited with more than 2.5 million deaths. The world had paused. And Momma had moved.

"It was something about us that that white man liked," Momma said, proud, talking again about the bank officer. He had signed off on the initial loan for the laundry center and offered to help secure a second loan to convert the laundry center into a rental duplex. Trading quarters for dollars. Momma and Daddy took him up on the offer.

In the five years between 1987 and 1992, Momma and Daddy converted the laundry center into a two-unit duplex, then expanded that two-unit duplex into a six-unit apartment complex, then sold the apartment complex and used the money to help them build a house—and the next part of their life together—in a town about forty miles south of where the laundry center stood. We moved into the house in 1994.

"When we first moved in, nothing was done," Momma said. "Nothing was completed. We had a shell of a house. Concrete floors with no rug. Sheetrock with no paint. No wallpaper. Bathrooms with no plumbing." Then her voice went from remembering to laughing. "We had a kitchen though. Had a stove in there because I had to cook. I *haaaad* to cook. Your daddy was gon' make sure I did that."

The house was big enough to hold all of our things: furniture, memories, Daddy's dreams and nightmares. We filled it up until we emptied out. In 2005, my brother graduated high school and decided to go to college in Tacoma, Washington, more than two thousand miles away. A couple of years later, I graduated high school and decided to go to college in St. Paul, Minnesota, more than a thousand miles away. The year after that, Daddy died of liver cancer. The house became Momma's house then. Her world became her world again. The stuff too.

"That's what my mind just kept coming back to," Momma said, reflecting on why it took years after Daddy's death to decide to sell the house. "All that stuff." Neither of us could remember whose idea it was. I thought the idea was mine. She knew it was hers. Maybe it was neither of ours. Maybe the idea came home one day by itself and just waited for Momma to find it. "This would have been in 2016." Her words trailed off and stayed a murmur for a while. Eventually I could hear her again. "I would look up and see all the stuff I would have to try and go through and get rid of it, or figure out what I'mma do with it. That's why I didn't sell it then."

"Two lives take up a lot of room," I said. We were still watching *Columbo*, both knowing what would eventually happen. The detective would figure it all out, and even the stuff that didn't make sense would.

There was a heavy, blue living room set that I can only remember sitting on one time, the day of Daddy's funeral. Momma said it was her favorite. There was something Momma called a hutch and another heavy piece of furniture with a knob and a hinged top that we both agreed to call a record player. The house had gotten both of those, and other things, from Grandma's house when she died, two weeks after Daddy, her son, did. Momma and Daddy had picked up other pieces of stuff too, all in pairs and sets in their early years together. A round kitchen table with a black marble top. A love seat. A sectional. Later on, Momma replaced the stuff my brother and I had taken from the house with her own touches, her own taste, using the imagination that Daddy had tried to take from her. She made everything how she wanted. She filled the rooms with bright colors and Bobby Womack, closets with wigs and purses, Saturday nights with champagne and Barry White. There were pictures everywhere too, framed and scaling the walls, folded and tucked into things not meant to hold them, in drawers and on countertops. And flowers, planted and growing around the house and out near the mailbox, and always on Mother's Day.

In the backyard, there was the storage building that Daddy built, where he used to get high and fix stuff. Further out, there was the shed that Daddy made my brother and me build. It was beside the fence he made us lay around the land, land that he made us cut and keep for the cows, cows that he made us watch, feed, sell, and chase for the money. It always seemed to come back to that.

It took four years—from 2016 to the seventh month of the pandemic—for Momma to want to sell the house at the same time somebody else wanted to buy it; and it took five months for us all to agree on what should happen to all the stuff inside.

I want to say I helped Momma. That's why I took a job that brought me back to Mississippi in 2016—to help. I want to say I went every weekend and moved things from upstairs to downstairs, from inside to a burn pile out back by the clothesline that Daddy used to grow his grapes. I want to say I lifted the heavy things for her and organized the important ones for us. I want to say I was there. But the pandemic made things go in reverse. A year seemed like ten. A week felt like it stretched on for months. One day was all the others. The best thing you could do for the people you wanted to be closest to was stay away.

I helped when I could, but Momma moved that house, just like she helped build the laundromat and a world for my brother and me to live in. She lifted and pushed. She piled and hauled. She packed and loaded. She climbed. "I did," she said, at sixty-one years old, "and when I finished, I went through every room, every single room, and stood or sat, and said I can't believe it. You did it. I told myself. I did it."

"And I touched everything. I touched the walls. I went over the closet doors. I talked as I was going through. I touched everything to let it know I was there. Then I laid down in the kitchen floor—Bruce's kitchen," she said, smiling. "My kitchen; and I remembered."

There Is a Daughter

Alice Walker

for Alexandria Ocasio-Cortez

there is a daughter
taking the floor
there is a daughter
standing in the light
of her mother's prayers,
her father's dreams,
her teachers' high hopes
as well as in the shadow
of our common disillusionment.

there is a daughter
speaking the truth
that lives in her heart.
there is a daughter
standing alone

taking care
of the Soul
that might have lived
all these years
—if not endlessly stoned—
in our House.

"I May Not Get There with You"*

Voting for those who could not, standing with those who know

for Stacey Abrams, Raphael Warnock, and Jon Ossoff

The Promised Land
Is the sound
From the Mountain Top
Of all our ancestors
Cheering us on.
If it is a place,
it is made
both of stubbornness
and soul.
A destination
That always was
within.

*MLK. Thank you for continuing the race.

Hello, Goodnight

Kamille D. Whittaker

Dad went back to Jamaica soon after something told Mom to come home early from her graveyard shift at the hospital and she found him drunk and covered in vomit on the kitchen floor. The smoke from two charred hot dogs in a saucepan billowed throughout our three-bedroom house, into my brother's room where he wheezed in his sleep, into the living room, where she found me crying in the broken swing that tremored like a kinked metronome.

The first time this happened, my brother, all of four or five years old, drew me from my crib and crawled with me to the front porch steps, where we waited with neighbors until the smoke cleared, as Mom barreled home mid-shift.

She eventually began shuttling us to my aunt's house each night before work—once Dad's dealings with us at home dribbled into fits of tenderness and remiss.

He'd pace in the den, lean and gangly, with hands on

narrow hips, in search of my blanket that had been washed so many times it was vanishing. He'd sit, surrounded by his vinyl, bass guitar, and electronics mangled in mounds of cables and wires, with my little red radio he promised to fix—forgotten like his pledge to come see me march around the school at our Halloween parade in Mrs. Lewis's first-grade class. I had dressed up as a bride that year; and Mom finally let me wear her rose clip-on earrings, a string of pearls, and hot pink lipstick out in public. I had sashayed down the school walkways, weaving through the upperclassmen courtyards and waving at teachers and friends who lined the hallways. I pictured Dad at the parade's end, a little twinkle in his eye.

When he didn't show, Mom and I picked him up at The Harbor, a bar tucked behind a Buddhist temple, where we had grown accustomed to collecting him on most days. We'd wait in our blue Ford Escort in silence until he meandered out of the dive's back door and collapsed in the passenger seat, giggling, incoherent, foul.

Rum and epileptic seizures drowned him in waves that pushed him further out of reach. A car crash up an embankment hurled him through the windshield and killed what we knew of him. When they wheeled him into the operating room that night—brain scrambled, face disfigured—they asked Mom to decide whether the slim chance at saving his life was worth the extraordinary measures it would require.

"I wish we could all be together again, sweetie," he started to say in a loop, after he returned home to Jamaica and the time between seeing him stretched until it puckered then sagged.

During summer and winter visits, I tried to gather the grand, shiny things I wanted to tell him about the past school year. I pictured how he might respond, how his eyes might light up, the questions he might ask.

"I know, Dad. I know," I'd respond instead; my own words, as years drifted into decades, were heaped and listless like ashes.

Dad had kind eyes that sparkled when he smiled and smooth skin the color of cassava root.

He had been a cost accountant by day, a DJ and bass player by night, and an electrician in between. He could fix anything, like our record player, so I could 'fro my hair out like old-school Whitney and belt out "Yeah! I wanna dance with somebody!" and dance on Mom's long center table that she'd polish with Pledge on Sundays.

"Le-*roy*," she would say, sucking her teeth and emphasizing the last syllable like Jamaican women do. In the syllable, a host of discontents. "Just pray for him, you hear?" she'd always add.

She'd find her way to dance with me, each time telling me about how she and Dad would follow reggae basslines in Spanish Town and Kingston dancehalls from night until dawn. She'd lower her chin and voice, mimicking the notes I'd never heard him play. She'd have a smile in her voice, and laughed until her eyes watered about this world of yesterdays that filled in all my blanks.

"My dad had stage four colon cancer. It spread to his liver. It was aggressive," I started to recite mostly out loud, mostly to myself, as the summer days folded into fall. It was around the time that *Vanity Fair* unveiled its September 2020 cover, with a police-downed Breonna Taylor bathed blue by artist Amy Sherald.

Socially distanced political conventions and tightened public health protocols signaled impending doom.

Summer started with a call from my aunt that Dad had gone

to the emergency room after losing consciousness and becoming severely anemic. It wasn't Covid. They ruled it out early on in his short stay, which included a blood transfusion. But the ordeal set into motion a series of tests, including a colonoscopy to forage for previously undetected bleeding. They saw the tumor then, and the beast had spread to the liver.

I repeated the refrain out loud as if it was a thing that already had occurred, so I could get used to speaking of him in the past tense and preempt the heavy of the present. I thought that if I came to early terms with his impending passing, I could muddy the process of grief just enough to throw it off my scent and scramble time. I could hedge against the muck of regret and longing.

"My dad died," I mouthed for the first time out loud sometime on the first day of October. More practice to ready myself for life after death. The three short words burned my throat as they gurgled up to my tongue. I shuddered, and only said it once. Any day now.

I rehearsed what I would say to the customs agent in Jamaica when the time came for her to look me up and down and sneer, "Who lives on Michelton Way? Linstead is outside of the safe corridors for Covid. You'll have to quarantine for fourteen days before you can…"

"My dad, Ma'am," I'd say.

"*Lived*," I'd correct.

During one conversation, when Dad was feeling like himself, I asked him, "What is something that you wanted to teach us, Dad, something that you feel you didn't get a chance to?"

"I'd tell you to be wise," he started without pausing, as if he was waiting for the question all along.

"Be…wise," I repeated as I hurried to scribble it down on the nearest piece of scrap paper.

"Be honest," he said next, this time, more slowly.

Be honest, I wrote.

"And to not hate…to always forgive."

"Al-ways…for-*give*," I repeated, and held the last syllable one beat, then two.

They sent him home from the hospital, hoping to firm him up for surgery and then chemotherapy and radiation.

They sent him home from the hospital to make him comfortable for the next big thing. Possibly to die.

In the strained conditions of some of Jamaica's public hospitals, overrun by Covid, there was no more room for him in the ward. In the second week of October, confirmed Covid cases in Jamaica had inched over 7,200 with 128 fatalities. Of the confirmed cases, nearly 90 percent were locally acquired and bloated the interior hospitals. If Dad stayed, he might have been exposed to further infection.

Back home, his legs had swelled with edema until he couldn't walk. His abdomen had become distended, and his skin was stained the color of urine.

He answered my call that evening, every evening, with "Hello, goodnight!" a linguistic quirk that Caribbean people, possibly only Jamaicans, have taken up—to both greet and say good-bye at the same time. The actual end of a call or conversation is less formal and perhaps intentionally muddled—a grunt, a simple "all right" or a promise of "more later" ("likkle more") for tomorrows that are not.

"Are you afraid, Daddy?" I asked him after he told me he was really sick. He still wouldn't say that it was cancer ravaging him, even though I had known. Saying it, I imagined, sounded too much like surrender.

In the pause that followed, I heard the background crackle of the radio that was always set to RJR 94 FM and was always on and always made it a chore to hear him clearly. Many summer evenings he sat, wide-legged and shifting his weight from one side to the other with his two elbows on his knees, hands clasped and ears close to the transmitter, captivated. He distilled his gatherings over a meal later.

Did you hear...?

Did you know...?

Did you see...?

"I am, Kam," he eventually replied. "I am a little afraid."

I wanted to pray with him and comfort him. I wanted to share with him another big, grand, shiny thing that would collapse the time and cruel distance. I wanted the words "I am too" to form and flood around me.

But the moment writhed and was anxious to pass.

And, so, I let it.

My aunt was weary. On October 13, Dad woke up and told his only sister that he wasn't feeling like himself. He had a "low feeling."

She called the ambulance and waited for it to make its way a few winding miles from Linstead Hospital, through Linstead Market, over the overgrown train tracks and around the bend to the light blue and white house with the speckled wrought-iron fence. It was the house with the orange tree that I sat under on many a summer day, where Dad peeled the oranges and I slurped up their sweetness, one after another.

He kept asking for water, a sign that his organs were failing, the doctor later informed us. First his kidneys, then his tumor-devoured liver. He had developed severe anemia, and in the end, his big, strong heart that had already evaded death once before could no longer shore up a surrendering body.

My aunt called his name over and over—Le-*roy*, Le-*roy*, Le-*roy*—she later told me over a phone connection that sputtered and frothed. But he couldn't stay awake. He drifted off to sleep before the ambulance came, and they could not re-suscitate him.

"I don't think he knew what was happening. He didn't know he was dying," she wailed over the call, her voice high.

"He knew, Auntie," I said. "He knew."

The body knows. There's a scar on my brother's brow, a smooth sliver of skin that the sun never bothered to stain. If he were reborn, the scar seemed to say, this is the hue he might be. And then no one would know how he swung back and forth on the speckled wrought-iron fence, free and flying, a beat too long after Mom warned him to stop and right before the holler.

When we were young and we would run and jump and play, his lungs would grip him. And then he would spend long eve-nings wheezing under He-Man covers, pushing thick breath out of angry pipes. From his room, I'd smell the Vicks and his inhalants misted by the humidifier that hummed low and cool until the grip went slack.

"Don't worry, he's going to be okay, love," Mom whispered to me.

Before she pulled his door closed, I saw him with his cheeks pressed against the praying hands that summoned me, a little sister specifically, into existence, into his world of magic and play and swinging on gates and chasing lizards and flight.

When the phone call came, I thought of his lungs—catchments where grief and longing seeped into the creases and folds, calling them home.

My aunt started speaking of duppies after the pandemic scut-tled plans for travel and tradition. A proper Jamaican send-off meant having a Nine Nights set-up, a celebratory bashment culminating a nine-night wake at the home of the departed.

Loved ones dance and chant and wail until the hollow on the inside feels full again.

If the body is not given a proper send-off, then the duppy will linger.

To keep the spirits away, I told her to paint the ceiling and the window trim on the veranda the blue I had seen from the Keys to the Carolinas—since spirits apparently don't traverse water or, it turns out, the color of it.

The urn that eventually cradled Dad's ashes and waited in vain for our arrival from the States and my sister's arrival from Barbados for a proper send-off was awash in it: two parts archipelago seawater to one part indigo—a kind of blue.

It's not the ending I rehearsed or practiced. I took up playing jazz piano this summer, reasoning that in the year of The Great Pause, I was squandering my gift.

I started from scratch, every day, first with scales, then chords. I practiced phrases that I would one day recite for Dad who, in all our years, never heard me play.

That kind of thing would *sweet* him—hearing the parts of me that he composed. And in my mind, that would be when and how I imagined, *needed* for the end, our end, to come.

A long day would puddle at Dad's feet. He'd be feeling "low" and needing to hear…peace, until the hollow on his inside felt full.

"Play me a song," I'd hear him whisper, his eyes heavy, nearly closed.

For a while, he'd trace my tune on the piano with a hum that cracked on the high notes and dipped low when his chest did. Eyes closed now.

And when the sleep finally came, only the silence, only the remains: he, father of the living; me, daughter of dust.

The Women Who Clean

Aunjanue Ellis-Taylor

A peephole. I look through it searching for permission. An empty hallway is what I need. Permission. Permission to go out into an empty world. I can't go yet. I see them. The lens contorts, fogs their bodies. I hear them. The women who clean. I can tell they are young. I can tell they are Black. They are there, so I will have to wait. I try to picture them based on their voices. I try to hear their gossip, their complaints. It's garbled. I wonder about these women. I wonder if they wonder about me and why, after days and days, I have not left the room.

I am protecting them. I am a walking contagion.

In January of 2020, I went to Los Angeles to begin filming a movie that would be my biggest job to date. A studio picture. Second lead to a megastar. For weeks I was blissed. I was doing work that I enjoyed. I loved my coworkers. Los Angeles was my playground. When I wasn't working, I was happily drowning in Betye Saar, Lauren Halsey, Gregory Porter, Raphael Saadiq. Dancing till early morn to a set DJed by Erykah Badu. My friend went with me to one of these events and said something about avoiding an Asian person because of a virus. I had no patience for this. (Still don't.) I told her so.

The megastar assured me the movie would not shut down. No one understood the gravity yet. I wanted to finish this job so I could get that check. Then one rainy Friday in March we were sent home early. The megastar said we would be back to work on Monday. We did not go back.

Afraid to travel, I decided to shelter in Los Angeles until things got better. I was afraid to order food, so for days I was starving and then my body started performing new tricks. Incessant coughing. Shortness of breath. Runny nose. I had to sit down after merely putting a sheet on my bed. There were times I was gasping for air. I rationalized my symptoms. I anticipated dying. And in the middle of this undiagnosed Covid trauma—there were no tests then—Los Angeles kept shaking. Earthquakes. I was sleeping in my car at night. I thought it was the safest place. My body recovered, but Los Angeles kept shaking. The virus didn't go away, so I packed my rental car and drove home to Mississippi listening to the Winans, Lianne La Havas, and Radiohead, peeing on the side of the road along the way.

On the road trip, I saw the politics of the virus. Every digital sign on Interstate 10 from California to New Mexico flashed WEAR A MASK! As soon as I got to Texas, signs said WEAR A SEATBELT! The closer I got to Mississippi, the more life seemed unchanged. Finally I made it home, back to my house and my family.

I was afraid to touch them. So I didn't.

In late September I returned to my dream job but a different world. I was tested three times a week. Sometimes twice in one day. The film shut down because six people tested positive, but the lab made a mistake. We went back to work.

Miracle of miracles I finished the movie virus-free. I drove back to Mississippi. I was in my house dancing on Chaka Khan's clouds feeling like a holy survivor and so glad, so glad to be home. And then I got a text from someone who had been in my home a couple of days before I returned, saying they tested positive. Everything they'd touched I had touched.

Days later, I couldn't wake up, my appetite was gone, and my nose was running like an unfixed faucet. I took a test, not because I thought I was sick, but just as a ceremonial precaution before I spent time with my family over Christmas. I knew that it would be negative like every other test—upwards of forty—I had taken over the past few months.

It was positive.

By that evening I am a shrine for offerings of cookies, jewelry, socks, balloons, soup my family leaves outside the window of the Hampton Inn room that I can't leave.

On the second day of my quarantine, the hallway is quiet; the Black women who clean have gone for the day. The French call quarantine *confinement*. It is the most apt word for how I feel—*confined*. Jailed. But they have gone, and my room is close to the exit. I can leave for my daily walk. Outside of my phone calls and TV, the Black women who clean are the only voices I hear. They are unaware but they keep me company.

By the fifth day of quarantine, I want to leave the room. The hotel sounds quiet. The hallway is clear. It is Christmas, so the women who clean have gone home to their families. I envy their freedom. I have attached faces to their voices. I miss them. I'm glad they aren't here.

I am reminded of another Black woman who cleans. Years

ago, one of my family members was hospitalized many times. She slept mostly, and so I spent a lot of time alone, listening and watching and wanting someone to talk to me to distract from my everyday horror.

Class and race were ever present. I never once saw a white woman or a white man clean the halls of the hospitals. Not once.

In line at a Subway after I left her sick room, I saw a white man drop his soda on the floor. A Black woman who cleans came with her mop and washed the spill. I watched him watch her do this. I watched him physically shrug his shoulders as he did. With those shrugged shoulders he seemed to be saying *What do you want from me?* My mouth dried with anger.

There is an economy in Mississippi dedicated to women who clean and give care or "sit." These women are—with little variation—Black women. These are professions that should be supported and elevated. But these professions should be chosen, not fallen into out of lack of choice. This lack of choice is a result of impoverished education—the poverty having little to do with money. This is no vestige of the slave economy. It's an absolute and intentional lack of investment in young Black women and girls. They care for and clean the messes of the elderly men and women who in their youth burned and bombed churches and lynched Black Mississippians. Some of the victims were family members of the women. I wonder about these women. I wonder if they wonder about me.

My quarantine is over. I have missed Christmas and New Year's with my family. I pay for the room for days after I leave, so that the Black women who clean won't enter it and be exposed to the virus that I still carry. Their voices, wraiths that still linger.

When I am home again, I don't feel much like a survivor. I didn't get horribly ill this time. I remain convinced that I had the virus back in March. My time with my family was stolen. I spray their gifts with Lysol before I can give them. I throw things away that I have touched so no one else will touch them. I can finally see my family without obstruction and not be an amiable zoo animal behind a window. I pray that soon I will feel safe enough to hold my niece's hand.

Days later, I get a text asking, "Are you watching?" I turn on the television and see the January 6 insurrection happening in real time. I refuse to devote space and type to this, but what I thought watching was this: What will happen when the cameras leave? Who will restore the House to order? Who will clean the blood off the floors? Who will pick up the trash left behind by these "this is our country" looters? I have no doubt Black women who clean will be there doing at least some of this work. I think of the man at the Subway with his shrugging shoulders: *What do you want from me? I'm a white man. This is your job. This is what you do. You clean up after me.*

Black women who clean. We are separated only by our stated occupations. I think of the soiled, diapered asses of elderly confederate men now in Mississippi. I hear them screaming "Change me. Change me!" I think of the work we are expected to do to engage with Proud Boys and QAnons to disarm them with our strategies of civil discourse and love. We are tasked with cleaning them, washing them of their anti-Black hatred, making them better men and women. I am Fannie-Lou-tired of the pain and labor of Black women acting in service of repairing white avarice and white destruction, of enabling white redemption.

There is other work calling me. Work that is in service of Black people, with economies and infrastructure that serve

see-through, but you have what it takes to see this through. Multitudes *are* seeing their own freedom through you. But if you study the sky through your quarantine window you will learn that you are not just the lens, you are the whole existence beyond it. Uncontainable as air.

In 2020 I conducted a sky study.* My study consisted of looking out my window after I meditated each morning and then writing a new revelation about my own interior life while pretending to describe the sky. The poems I wrote were not necessarily haiku in form, their syllables and numbers of lines varied day by day based on what the sky was teaching me. But they are in the lineage of daily practice that Sonia Sanchez invited us all into with her morning haiku—her daily peace haiku. And of course they are in the tradition of the Japanese nature poets who created a poetic technology for being in the moment with nature. The poems I am sharing here are poems from August. They are acts of Black liberation made possible by the revolutionary ancestors Malcolm X Grassroots Movement invites us to celebrate every August. I am sharing the poems that converge with the collective Black August Haiku practice Durham North Carolina's SpiritHouse sparked a decade ago. The overlap reminded me that these poems, created in a particularly comfortable solitary condition, are part of a collective breathing that honors many ancestors, including those whose names we do not know, but whose brave actions make our existence possible. Invisible. Crucial. Like air.

*It was not grant funded. But it was peer-reviewed in the sense that three months after I started I began emailing the poems to my dear sister friend Yashna Maya Padamsee.

a blue
   so thick
you can
   shape it

breathe

August 13, 2020

I am practicing, shaping my grief. The blue feeling of loss as big as the sky. The way loss can be a world without end especially in the absence of familiar rituals of recognition and closure, especially when we are removed from the tangible embrace of the living, those loved ones who grieve alongside us in separate rooms. My experience of grief is a thickness of air. I feel the molecules moving through me, condensing into salt water. My experience of grief is urgent. I can't take my breathing for granted, because you were breathing and where are you now?

Sitting, studying the sky I remember that like our breathing, the sky is never neutral. We have never been neutral. We consist of the many shapes of air. We are the way that air becomes visible in collectivity, in transition. This air of my screaming, my sobbing, my sigh, what does it collect? What collects me? This propulsion of my heaving, my heartbreak, my heat, where is it moving me? This sound of my tangible, torn-apart truth, what is it teaching me?

Grief, or the impossible-to-ignore evidence of how much I love you, is subject to the thermodynamic law of distillation. This humid breath of mine remembers the rain. Grief is the thickest form of love, so I let it reshape me. And yet breathing without you feels like a betrayal. How can I remember that even letting go is love?

> your breathing
>   feels like air
>   and looks like
>   light

August 11, 2020

You are the ones who teach me what breathing is for. Why I am shuttling this air. You are the reason to breathe down into my belly, this internal choreography of home. You are the ones I want to sing with. You are the reason it matters that I make these words soft enough to hold you, loud enough to carry.

We shouldn't have to teach the world about the sacredness of Black breathing. We shouldn't have to breathe ourselves back from the trigger of traumatic violence. We shouldn't have to bear the death toll of a country in denial. We shouldn't have to justify our need to pause and take a breath amidst so much adaptation.

But if we must rededicate our breathing (and we must), may we do it with our laughter. May we sing the songs of how free we feel together across it all. May we shine a light with where and how we choose to breathe. May we offer light and lightness of being to each other abundantly and first and again.

I had to study the sky because I had to reclaim my breathing. Not in response to the news cycle, but in communion with something bigger. I had to look at the clouds because I had to remember how to witness and believe in massive change. I had to study the sky because I had to teach myself to value my breathing, not on the terms of equality with white capitalist breath, but on the scale of the universe my breathing creates and recreates again now.

a storm
   is a mountain
      you live inside

a life
   is a continent
      you breathe

August 4, 2020

A Survivor Looks Back

Lolis Eric Elie

How did I survive the pandemic?

I knew one day you would ask that question. Even now, this long after the worst ravages, I don't know that I can answer.

I know this: even as the virus began making its leap from animals to humans, people thought it couldn't happen; therefore, it wasn't happening. People could never be that savage to each other.

Even that is a lie, and the epidemiologists knew it.

We took consolation where we could. When one theory of solace had to be abandoned because it brought us neither safety nor comfort, we simply traded it for another.

At first we felt safe, because the disease was occurring far away and therefore could not affect us directly. Then the virus hit home via video screen. The nation and the world watched on repeat as a man named George Floyd struggled for more than nine minutes, clinging to life, begging for life, then losing life as the knee of the virus held fast its grip on the poor man's neck.

In that moment we lost our innocence. We thought, If the virus could do that to him, then could it not do the same to me?

That graphic tragedy spurred us from angry acceptance into action. While many cowered behind locked doors and semipermeable masks for protection, hundreds and thousands of people took to the streets, risking life and liberty in their determined fight for a cure. We had hope then because even though we knew there were small pockets of social scientists here and there working on policies that might one day fell this virus, never before had so many people been willing to risk everything in the singular effort to do to the virus what it had done so mercilessly to so many of us.

The authorities warned us to stay home. They said we should leave this fight to the experts and not take matters into our own hands. But they had no credibility, having so consistently failed to develop even a semblance of solution. We knew our only hope was with each other.

Even that hope was short-lived.

It was as if the authorities were in cahoots with the virus itself, each in turn attacking the most heroic among us specifically for their determination to rid the world of that troublesome plague.

In Denver, the authorities gassed people. Elisabeth Epps, a member of the Denver Police Department's Use of Force Committee, resigned that post after she was shot by police projectiles. In Houston, authorities on horseback trampled a woman. In New York, officers continued to beat people with clubs, even after they had already been felled to the ground. In Columbus, they pepper sprayed Congresswoman Joyce Beatty.

When confronting any enemy, the human impulse is to imagine our enemy as ourselves. That's what we did. Imagined that, even as it spread to pandemic proportions, this virus would respond to our efforts as we ourselves would respond when facing an adversary like us. Sunlight is the best disinfectant, the old folks say. That adage gained new traction in those desperate times. There was no science behind it, yet we believed it. We had faith that if we could expose the virus by capturing video images of people succumbing to its terrible ravages, then the virus, like we ourselves, would cower in the face of exposure and cease to spread.

We learned that that's not the way this contagion worked.

In Salt Lake City, during a live newscast, police shoved an elderly man to the pavement as he walked with his cane. In Chicago, outside Brickyard Mall, police were filmed smashing a car's windows and forcibly extracting its occupant. In city after city, the authorities targeted journalists as if to make a mockery of our conviction that the plague wouldn't dare be so bold if evidence of its atrocity was documented.

In San Jose, Officer Jared Yuen, policing frontline heroes amassed in the street, said, "Shut up bitch" to one and "Let's get this motherfucker" of another. The reaction? Eddie Garcia, Yuen's police chief, kept him on the force and later said he regretted if his response to Yuen's actions seemed "cavalier." Garcia then went on to be appointed the chief of police in Dallas.

We retained our faith, if not in authority, then in science. Science, after all, had explained to us that these isolated instances of sudden death and injury were indeed related, were not merely a virus but a pandemic. What we were tempted to see as a viral problem in one corner of the world was a pandemic affecting the globe. Then came what was perhaps the worst news: the virus was capable of mutating. Even before we could stop it as it was, it was fast becoming something else.

We had believed that it attacked mostly the respiratory

system. We had seen George Floyd's breathing give out on video.

We learned that three months before Floyd's death, the virus had claimed another victim in much the same way in Altadena, California. A video had captured Edward Bronstein repeatedly crying out "I can't breathe" as California Highway Patrol Officer Dusty Osmanson and several of his colleagues pinned Bronstein to the ground, killing him. A few months before the Bronstein killing, we discovered evidence in Paris that Cédric Chouviat, a forty-two-year-old Frenchman of North African descent, had been suffocated in a similar way— dying of asphyxia and a broken larynx.

We thought we knew this to be a disease that attacked the throat, the lungs. We did not know it to also be a disease of the eyes.

In Minneapolis, the writer Linda Tirado was blinded in one eye. In Dallas, Brandon Saenz had his left eye shattered. In Omaha, Adam Keup was struck in the right eye by two pepper balls. In La Mesa, Leslie Furcron, a fifty-nine-year-old grand-mother, lost sight in one eye after being hit by a "beanbag" shot by police.

The version of the virus that attacked the eyes came to be known as the Chilean variant, so named because it was so prominent among protesters in that country. More than two hundred victims there were afflicted in that way. In France, members of the gilets jaunes who had sought a cure for that country's virus variants were said to have lost twenty-four eyes and even five hands in their collective struggle to defeat the contagion.

In Israel, the variant of the virus was a disease of Palestinian knees. FORTY-TWO KNEES IN ONE DAY a headline in *Haaretz* declared, detailing the price exacted from people fighting for an end to the contagion there.

It was soon everyone for himself in developing a personal strategy for salvation. Some thought that by locking their doors and taking to their beds, they could safely outlive the virus. Realists (damn them!) pointed out that Breonna Taylor had been tucked beneath the cozy sheets of her bed, behind the locked door of her apartment, the night she died.

Some people placed their trust in colors. If you just dressed in blue, mirroring the color of the virus itself, you would be protected, they said. In St. Louis, Luther Hall was savagely beaten down by the virus though he himself was one of the boys in blue.

"Green! Army green! That's the color of prophylaxis!" green's partisans declared. But in Virginia, Caron Nazario, an army lieutenant dressed in the green camouflage of his profession, learned in a hail of threats and pepper spray that he was no more immune than anyone else.

White skin—that was the talisman that most often seemed to ward off the virus. But it was almost impossible to obtain in the secondary market, and even those who were born with it would sometimes find themselves injured or worse if they dared place their bodies near the front lines of the battle for a cure.

Mechell Hensler learned this in Fort Wayne.

She wasn't in the streets to protest police murder and misconduct, but perhaps she should have been. She and her daughter got tear-gassed by police just like all those citizens who were in the Fort Wayne streets that day to march against oppression by law enforcement. She explained to one of the cops that her daughter was only three years old and the gas had forced them from their vehicle. The innocence of her explanation seemed only to incite him to further violence. He threw a canister of tear gas that exploded in the child's face. Just when a kind stranger came to the child's aid and was able to coax a smile from her with a cough drop, the second canister exploded.

My son, your mother and I took our solace in the fact that children seemed to be immune to the virus. Even as adults were told to hide behind masks and keep our distance, we were also told that children, by some strange quirk of nature, were thought to be virtually virus-proof.

You were three years old then. But you were willful, inclined to push anything or anyone that got in the way of you doing what you wanted to do. Your doctor said you were in the ninetieth percentile for height. You were a dark child like your grandfathers. Would your youth protect you from a disease that your size and color rendered you especially susceptible to? At what age would adultification bias strip white people of their ability to see you and dark children like you as children?

Sometimes in those days, you would toss and turn or even wake in your bed as if accosted in your sleep by some terrible vision. Were you dreaming of tear gas and pepper spray? Of virus and violence? I would sleep with you then, providing whatever comfort I could. And in those wee hours it seemed that we have always been in pandemic times of one kind or another. But perhaps it wouldn't always be thus. I thought that if only I could keep you alive through that current unpleasantness, then perhaps from the loins of your son's son's daughter's daughter, a cure for this terrible virus might emerge.

I thought that if I could survive long enough to keep you alive, then there might be hope that we as a people could outlive these wars and the wars to come. This is the faith to which I held fast.

Oh. How did I survive the pandemic?

I was lucky.

Iron and Brass

Rosalind Bentley

"This is a story, not a contribution to historical research."
—Sven Lindqvist, *Exterminate All the Brutes*

My wife and I moved into our dream home on Thanksgiving Day 2019, three months before the country shut down. We'd stalked the neighborhood for five years, cruised its broad streets, admired the mid-century homes that rambled and sprawled just enough to suggest graciousness rather than excess. Peering at them from our car windows, we imagined the Saturday morning back and forth between us over whose turn it was to cut the grass, which, given each lawn's size, would warrant one of us serving the other a well-earned beer or two when the task was done.

Early in our search, one house came up for sale, twice. If you could have seen that kitchen. Spanking new countertops rolled like runways. Perfect for scattering a mess of freshly picked collard greens grown in the garden we'd plant in the backyard, or for rolling out dough for cherry pie, a magic my wife conjures at holidays. A small, built-in bar beckoned at one end where we'd stir cocktails. Upstairs needed work, lots of it, but why let that stop a dream?

Both times the house hit the market, we bid on it. The first time, I wrote a letter to the owner because she was from Marianna, seat of my family's ancestral homeland, Jackson County, Florida. Certainly, an appeal to the homegirl connection would win the day. It didn't. Money did, but not ours. Both times we lost to people with pockets deep enough to pay cash and do the upstairs reno outright.

So, a few years later, when we finally did get a house (a different one but on the same street!) and walked through the doors that Thanksgiving Day, we couldn't believe our good fortune. The place was turnkey. Patches of oak floors, not smothered by our moving boxes, gleamed in sunlight. Creamy bare walls stood ready to embrace our art. New plumbing and wiring snaked through the hidden spaces that really matter, the guts of the house, pumping water to the gleaming bathrooms and filling the dining room with warm, welcoming light from the chandelier. And the kitchen. This was a collard-greens kitchen, a cherry-pie kitchen, a both-dishes-being-made-at-the-same-time kitchen. Honed soapstone countertops, plenty of cabinets, bookshelves for my cookbooks. My only bourgeois lament was that the previous owners omitted a pot filler over the cooktop when they remodeled.

Spring 2020 promised house-proud dinners, brunches, and cocktail parties with friends. Some real George and Weezy Jefferson, moving-on-up-type living. Yet, the new year dawned and news segments about a virus spreading in China soon shifted to twenty-four-hour coverage of world-wide sickness, fear, and immeasurable loss. The house is near a hospital. As the thunder from air ambulances grew more and more frequent each day, we knew things were getting worse. Shelter in place, they told us. We were fortunate; we could. But, with each day of lockdown, each Netflix marathon and take-out meal for two eaten from Styrofoam containers (thoroughly wiped down with sanitizing wipes after touchless front-door delivery), our forever home grew into something else. It became a reminder of who and what got us here—got me here—to this place of enormous privilege, protection, and shelter. A testament to the fear, pain, endurance, and hope that willed my family into existence.

I sit in the family room gazing at the backyard beyond the French doors. Mammoth pine trees cast dappled shade and a firepit surrounded by cedars and Adirondack chairs beckon up a small hill. Squirrels won't give the cardinals room at the bird feeder. The pool looks like a relic from a decommissioned Howard Johnson hotel, circa 1980, but the water is clear and a great relief on sweltering days.

Through the French doors, beyond the herb garden we planted for seasoning and pandemic sanity, I can see a cast-iron washpot I placed as an accent in the garden. Once jet-black, it now has a thin coating of rust that makes it look ashy. When I look at the iron belly, I think of a story told many times during my extended family's all-night rounds of bid whist at my aunt's house outside Marianna in Jackson County. The tale is as indelible a mark on my childhood as the fishing lessons my aunts gave me on the shore of our back-woods pond. Families are their stories, both fact and lore. The utterings bind. They fill where the "official" record gapes. For Black families, especially—people whose ancestors were often legally barred from learning to read and write—the stories are sometimes all we have.

The iron pot was my maternal great-great-grandmother's. She hauled water on my family's North Florida farm, filling the cauldron and heating it outside over an open flame. In it she churned clothes clean, most likely with a large wooden paddle powered by the strength of her dark brown arms, hands, and back. She washed on land my ancestors bought acre by acre after emancipation, selling their own eggs, corn, beef, and cotton until they'd amassed three hundred acres. Those strong arms and hands of hers also delivered babies, Black and white, on farms along their small stretch of the Chattahoochee River. I'd like to think she was paid to bring life into this world. But, as my relatives told it, her gift would be disrespected in a vile and common way.

Great-great-grandma Wooten, or "Maw," as she was called, was born in Virginia about the time Frederick Douglass was pressing Abraham Lincoln to issue the Emancipation Proclamation. At least one record says she was born in 1861, the year the great war over the autonomy of Black bodies began. Another says 1863, when she would have been born free. Whether she was brought to Jackson County, Florida, as an enslaved infant or a liberated child is unclear. But her legacy began in the Panhandle.

As a young woman she took a husband named Offie. They farmed, though I'm struck by a census entry listing her occupation as "none." In her lifetime, Maw midwifed my seven beloved great-aunts, my one great-uncle, and my grandmother. Maw's hands pulled my mother from the womb. So too with Mama's older sister, Mable, and their brother, Aldric. Quilts that kept the children warm were pieced together by Maw's nimble fingers. They gripped her waist when she'd get the spirit at Macedonia Missionary Baptist Church, up the road from the farm. Aunt Mable often recalled how Maw, overcome with the Word or a hymn, paced the aisles between the pews shouting, "Glor-EE! Glor-EE!" In telling that part of the story, Aunt Mable always mimicked Maw's strut, a memory from her own childhood watching Maw's black, Edwardian-style lace-up boots pound the church's plank floors. Perhaps

Maw raised her voice in joyful release. Perhaps as a cry of deliverance.

One day circa 1882 or 1884, Maw was called out to deliver a white woman's baby. The woman's husband came by wagon to gather Maw, whose own husband was away for a stretch of months. Why was he gone? I tell myself it doesn't matter. What matters is people knew Offie wasn't around.

Was it a difficult birth? Was it easy? Did the baby thrive? Was it stillborn? Did Maw tie the cord off with the strip of cotton like one she stitched onto her quilts? Here is the telling that matters most, the one her descendants have rendered as fact. On the way back to her cabin, the farmer attacked Maw. In one moment, she was bringing another body into the world; the next, she wasn't able to protect her own.

What we know for sure is the rape of Black women is a narrative of the antebellum South. It did not stop once Black people were liberated. Florida enacted some of the earliest and most stringent laws aimed at keeping Black people in ostensible bondage almost immediately after the war for their freedom ended. Called "black codes," the statutes were direct descendants of "slave codes" regulating all manner of free Black life. Vagrancy laws allowed an "unemployed" Black person to be arrested, jailed, fined, and then relegated to peonage to a white person. As historian Joe M. Richardson wrote in his 1968 paper examining Florida's black codes, selling "leaf tobacco or cotton without evidence of ownership" could land a Black man behind bars. (Almost 150 years later, selling loose cigarettes on a New York City street would cost a Black man his life at the hands of police.) The state legislature restricted Black men's right to vote. Seemingly, any exercise of their freedom, any action deemed a demonstration of "not knowing their place" was codified as a crime. Is that why Offie was missing?

Should a Black man be accused of assaulting a white woman, the codes sanctified his death. For the assault of a Black woman by a white man, there were no such penalties, legal or extralegal.

Nine months later, on Christmas Day, my great-grandmother was born. Not long after, Maw's husband, Offie, returned. I have a picture of Maw, her skin rich and dark. Aunt Mable said Offie's complexion matched his wife's. Which makes what he supposedly did upon seeing the fair-skinned baby with soft, wavy hair cradled in his wife's arms all the more remarkable. If I heard it once during one of those bid whist parties, I heard it a hundred times: Offie said, "What's born under this roof is mine." His land. His wife. Their child. A legacy to build together that no outsider could tear asunder.

And so, their daughter grew up and married my great-grandfather. They reared my grandmother and her sisters and brother to know the value and power of landownership and education. I am the beneficiary of those lessons. An acquaintance who grew up in the Midwest would smirk when she told me what her family said about fellow Black people who left the South during the Great Migration, but couldn't shed their rural ways: "Country as the day they left."

My childhood weekends were often spent walking along the dusty edges of family fields that were by then long dormant. I'm sure my love of Baby Ruth candy bars and Coca-Cola came from the shelves and cooler of my great-grandfather's rickety roadside store before it closed for good. And when Maw's granddaughter, who we called "Aunt Tee," opened her own country store on a dirt road closer to town, never once did I walk inside without hearing her beckon me: "Baby, get anything you want."

I learned to catch mullet with a cane pole in a couple of ponds dotting the remaining acres of my family's homestead.

I gathered bouquets of weeds I thought were wildflowers, and my aunts proclaimed them pretty. I fired my first gun on our land. The live oak trees, the tangles of bushes, even the scrub pines—how did those things and people like mine and legacies like Maw's become pejoratives?

Just as important as the stories we tell are the artifacts we pass down. They are reminders of storms weathered, of faith that landed me on this shore. In this dream house, in the midst of a worldwide nightmare.

My mother came up from Florida on move-in day to help us get settled. The virus was probably already here, silently ending plans, dreams, lives. We couldn't see it, so we acted on what was right in front of us—wave after wave of cardboard boxes.

Buried inside were articles of my family's belief in the future: the brass school bell my aunts rang outside the church that doubled as my mother's elementary school. Those aunts—Maw's granddaughters and great-granddaughter—were my mother's teachers, graduates of Tuskegee Institute and Florida Normal and Collegiate Institute. They frowned on me when I didn't immediately get my graduate degree after undergraduate school as they had. Decades later, when I finally got my MFA, even though they had passed away, I knew my aunts were still not pleased it took me so long to get an advanced degree. Still, I felt their pride. A box marked only as MASTER BEDROOM held quilts, some stitched by Maw and her daughter, some by my grandmother and her sisters. Generations later the stitching remains tight and fine, the cloth soft from keeping Maw's grandkids warm. There were many more quilts once, in Maw and Offie's old house. Years ago, when my uncle's mind was free from the scourge of dementia, he'd relive the day, when he was a little boy, that his cousins and aunts tore across the field to Maw's house. His eyes would flicker with the memory of the searing heat from the flames and the acrid scent of billowing smoke. He and his mother, Maw's first granddaughter, got there just as Maw was about to risk another run into the blaze to retrieve whatever she could. That granddaughter, the woman who would become my grandmother, held Maw back.

In time, the embers cooled. What remained of Maw's life as a free woman was rendered char.

The family built her another house nearby—small, of rough-hewn wood. The patch of land where the old home stood became a hogpen. She fed the pigs daily, and sometimes my uncle went with her. What must it have been for her to watch swine root around bits and pieces of her life, that were, by then, probably buried beneath a layer of dirt?

Maybe that's why one day as she approached with a bucket of swill, "she just fell on her knees and started praying." Whether silent or a whisper, the cause of her supplication was hers alone to know.

This makes me wonder about the andirons in our current fireplace. True to the sellers' disclosure, it is wood burning and in good working order. Andirons from the farmhouse where Maw delivered my mother, not the house that burned, now stand sentinel in our hearth. Were they salvaged from the rubble of Maw's house, a home that likely sheltered her through the outbreak of her time, the 1918 influenza pandemic? Aunt Mable became custodian of some farm heirlooms, including the bell and cauldron, when she built her own house a few miles outside of Marianna. For years she kept it outside, largely forgotten and eventually almost swallowed in a swale. Before she died ten years ago, I asked Aunt Mable if I could have it. "Sure, baby," was the answer. "That was Maw's old pot. But what you gon' do with it?"

My wife and I brought it to the dream home ourselves in her SUV. We'd used it as a makeshift firepit at our former home. That's no longer necessary, so it will find a new purpose. The sight of it fills me with guilt and gratitude.

Millions of people were nearly rendered homeless because of this pandemic. Food pantries fed hundreds of thousands who could not make ends meet because the shutdown meant they couldn't work. Grocery store clerks, bus drivers, nursing home aides risked their lives day in and day out because working from home was not an option. But I could, because of Maw and Offie.

The rust scales coating the cast-iron belly remind me of the enormous privilege their suffering and perseverance have granted me. Because of them, I earned a solid education, enjoyed a long, stable career, and now live in a beautiful home in which to ride out "these uncertain times," as they say. The peal of the brass school bell, still clear and true, reminds me that my achievements are forever tethered to a one-room schoolhouse along an unpaved country road. That schoolhouse was actually the church where Maw cried out on Sundays. The cauldron reminds me that I am the descendant of violence and horror. And yet, so, too, am I the product of love and hope.

Now that my wife and I are vaccinated, we'll plan a pool party. We'll open the French doors so people, also vaccinated, can mill in and out. There will be music and laughter and steaks sizzling on the grill. Maybe we'll scoop charcoal from the washpot. Or maybe fuchsia and lime coleus leaves will trail down its sides. The bathroom will be spotless and supplied with pretty paper hand towels and an overpriced scented candle, and we'll actually let people inside to use it. Something we didn't do the couple of times we tried to entertain outdoors before we had our shots. Guests were advised to wear masks and pee before they got here because we weren't letting them inside. That indignity may have kept us safe, but it made me feel like a discourteous host with no home training.

I'd also like to make a trip down to the church cemetery, about a mile from the homestead. My mother, named after Maw, recently had new headstones installed atop the graves of long-passed relatives. I haven't seen the markers yet, but apparently the current church pastor said they spruced up the whole graveyard, which is spare on shade trees, but usually overrun with faded plastic flowers.

The elements had nearly etched the oldest markers clean of any trace of who lay there beneath the anthills and sandy earth. My mother had Maw's new stone etched with the years of her birth and death along with these words: JULIA WOOTEN: MOTHER, GRANDMOTHER, AND MIDWIFE.

The truth of a tremendous life.

To Brim with Wholeness

Jasmin Pittman Morrell

My coughing bent me over the bathroom sink, gurgling up strands of blood that stained the porcelain red. The pain cinched a band around my lungs and kept me hunched into myself, unable to draw a full breath. The feeling was worse than childbirth. At least when I gave birth, I knew what to expect. I could always manage to breathe my way through the kind of pain that comes with knowing.

On that day in February, CNN reported that 1,770 people around the world had died from something called a "novel coronavirus." I'd never heard of Dr. Anthony Fauci before—why would I have reason to know the director of the National Institute of Allergy and Infectious Diseases? He told a news anchor from *Face the Nation* that we tumbled toward a global pandemic. I wondered if the virus could be successfully contained.

That day was a Sunday, and my husband begged to take me to urgent care.

"Let's wait a little while longer," I said. "It's probably nothing."

I didn't know how to explain my hesitancy, the fear of my pain being dismissed because of the brandy hues of my skin. He is a white man. He hadn't heard; even the goddess of tennis Serena Williams almost died from blood clots after giving birth in the hospital. Williams explained in an article written for CNN that her medical team did not immediately listen to her concerns, doubting her knowledge of her own body. I'd been sick for weeks with a teasing fever and simmering fatigue, my body's way of alerting me. If I didn't listen to it, who else would? I relented and decided to let him take me to the clinic. The fear released itself like a curled leaf falling from a tree, landing, then floating canoe-like down the French Broad River.

At the clinic, signs tacked to the wall asked patients if we'd recently been out of the country, warning of this new virus. We all seemed to lean away from each other, already vigilant against the slightest brush of skin against skin even if we didn't know yet to wear a mask.

When the doctor called me back to the examination room, my husband, Mike, came with me, his whiteness a talisman. The doctor's eyes mirrored his concern. She guided her stethoscope across my chest and down my back, asking me to take deep breaths that would not come.

"It's unlikely," she said, "but I'm sending you to the emergency room to be tested for a pulmonary embolism. You could have blood clots in your lungs," she explained. "If the clots travel to your brain or heart, it could be fatal."

You could leave your daughters motherless, I chastised myself for waiting so long to receive medical care. Before we left the girls with Mike's mother at our house, at least I'd made sure they heard the words "I love you."

I found myself talking to trees once I came back home from the hospital, particularly the river birches and weeping willow in my yard. Certain I'd fallen in love and perhaps even lost my mind a little, I allowed my secret guilt to nest in their limbs. I'd escaped death, even as this growing virus began to claim so many other lives—more than twelve thousand people world-wide at that time. I asked the trees for protection, thinking, *We're not out of the woods yet*, and then, *Look at you, cracking jokes with trees*. I felt guilt too for the sudden eruption of laughter escaping my lips, almost as though I'd been caught giggling during a funeral.

We were confined to an iridescent, intangible bubble—Roy Cooper, the governor of North Carolina, had declared it—and I couldn't imagine living through quarantine without these people of my blood and my heart alongside me. My family, my way of knowing. I saw a friend's Instagram post, an eerie shot of empty, sun-kissed San Francisco streets, her caption detailing what it was like to shelter in place. She noted how lonely she might've felt without being able to sit down to dinner with her roommates, who routinely found flowers on their shared table. I liked the phrase shelter-in-place, even if in San Francisco it was issued, somewhat menacingly, as an order.

I gave myself permission to receive shelter from my place, to take refuge in my home and my body. I signed up for a CSA (community-supported agriculture) delivery service to avoid going to the grocery store and also to support more local farms. The season sang its abundance in notes of rhubarb, bok choy, asparagus, and strawberries. And later, the crescendo of sugar plums and peaches called for crafting a galette my family devoured in moments. Our neighbor left a bag of cherry tomatoes fresh from the market on my doorstep, and even after making salsa, I had more than I needed.

I found a yoga teacher on YouTube and appreciated the way her guidance dripped honey down my spine. I even signed up for a virtual boot camp with a young, Black trainer. His dimpled smile was contagious, and I thought, Why not enjoy looking at this beautiful man? Mike just laughed at me as I sank into a squat.

I scheduled Zoom calls with old college friends, friends I didn't talk to often even before the pandemic, but now the need for connection felt urgent, vital. They reminded me of nights spent, all of us tipsy from cheap wine, sprawled in the grass on the lawn of our school's observatory, holding hands and staring up at the stars. Together, we practiced remembering more carefree days, when our lives stood before us, open and ripe, begging us to taste their sweetness. I knew my health depended on these things; I knew it like I'd never really known it before.

I lived in a historically Black neighborhood in Southern Appalachia, a region America does not imagine containing historically Black neighborhoods. Only about a mile away from our house, one of the country's first African American cultural halls still stood on Eagle Street, the building a totem for me and my neighbors. After police officers murdered Breonna Taylor and George Floyd and sparked nationwide protests, I wanted to join the ranks of those marching in our city streets, but fear of the virus overrode my sense of powerlessness and rage. So instead of joining others, I took a walk through our neighborhood, pushing my youngest daughter in her red jogging stroller, and noticed all of the BLACK LIVES MATTER signs in our yards. And then, there on the sidewalk was a perfectly spray-painted portrait of Breonna Taylor. I stopped as tears blinded my eyes. "Breonna," I said aloud, hoping no one ever has cause to say my daughters' names like that. I stepped off the sidewalk, refusing to push the stroller across her face. I ran the rest of the way home in the street, pushing all sixtyish pounds of my daughter and her stroller, grateful for the sweet burn in my legs and the celebration of honeysuckled air rushing in through my nose and down the column of my throat.

The cancer in my mother's bones brought her to us, to the mountains, far from the palm trees and sandhill cranes she adored. In the middle of a pandemic, it seemed impossible for diseases like cancer to exist concurrently, but just as summer brought its abundance, the crone of death appeared in all her usual guises. For her, we prepared to move across town into a bigger house, aided by a community of masked friends. The Mercy Movers, a volunteer group from our church, were willing to carry box after box in the heat and play Tetris with our belongings in the U-Haul. We tried to give each other a wide berth as we passed in tight spaces like the hallway or stairwell. I stationed bottles of hand sanitizer everywhere, a small mercy I could offer in return.

I mourned leaving Southside and its Blackness, an ode and a living presence.

But I could not let my mother take death's hand without standing beside her, offering my hand to clasp as well.

In January of 2021, I met a shaman at a retreat center tucked away just north of town, attempting to banish some of the year's grief now written into my cells. He was a friend, and he had reached out to me over the holidays to offer support, wondering if a retreat laced with ceremony could serve as a balm. The shaman carefully curated this group of five. We'd all tested negative for the virus. It was the first time I gathered with strangers, in person, in over a year. I was there for stillness and meditation. For rituals known to indigenous Andeans to ease ailments of body and spirit. For my mother, who now only visited me in my dreams.

We began inside the house, sitting on the floor in a room with plush carpet and pale morning light haunting the windows. During the opening circle, the shaman invited us to share any intentions we held for the retreat.

"I want to heal unprocessed grief," I heard myself say when my turn came, but I knew it was too soon for that. It had only been three months since my mother died. The U.S. alone had surpassed twenty million cases of the virus, and at that point, no one I knew was eligible to receive the vaccine. Mike's father tested positive. He would survive, but later that month, my mother-in-law would not.

Then there were things I couldn't speak, things only my body could articulate and perhaps needed to be blown away, the way a child blows away a delicate cloud of dandelion seeds.

After everyone around the circle spoke, the shaman invited us to go outside and explore the eleven surrounding acres of wooded hills studded with small stone altars. As I shrugged into a black puffer vest and headed outdoors, I caught a glimpse of myself in the mirror, and paused, unrecognizing. With red-rimmed eyes and sallow skin, there was something about the visibility of my grief that pleased me.

Wandering into a grove of trees on the property, I found a statue of the Buddha sitting cross-legged on the ground. I'd never met Buddha before, but as I sat and looked into his face, his openhanded presence soothed my mind. "Empty yourself," he seemed to say. He was a center of gravity, and after what felt like hours, I stood up, lighter than before. An eastern hemlock at the top of a hill looked like a welcoming place to spread my blanket underneath its branches. I lay on my back and watched its needles sway in the wind. The ground cradled me.

Eventually, the other two women on the retreat climbed the hill and sat gently, nymphlike, beside me. They wrapped their arms around me. They stroked my hair. "We know," they murmured. They'd lost parents too. Across the field, oaks, sweetgums, yellow poplars, and maples raised barren arms in reverence.

When night settled, our group gathered around a fire, no longer strangers. I learned none of the others who sat beside me were native to the South. They marveled at the way rhythms of this place can feel languid and the hospitality, lush. I'm lucky, no, I'm blessed, to have spent my life with this knowing. Silently, I thanked the Eastern Band of Cherokee for knowing more of this land than any of us ever would.

The fire's flames warmed and loosened the tight cords of muscles knotted in my shoulders. I wondered if this is what poet-warrior Audre Lorde had in mind when she wrote about self-preservation. I tilted my head to the stars and watched them dancing. Laughter echoed around me, but I was too full to laugh. I let bliss sink deep into all the parts and pieces of me that needed its light. Having grown up in the Church, the familiar words of Holy Communion reminded me: *this is my body, broken for you.*

But I am not broken open in sacrifice. My ancestors did not bring me here for that. Now is the time to brim with wholeness.

November 7, 2020

Samaa Abdurraqib

The air was surprisingly warm and the sky was that smooth,
    clear kind of blue.
Last warm day of the year hit brightly.
It was a Saturday.

Everyone had been holding their shoulders up for longer than
    any systems
could measure,
so the air was full of gasps of release.
Car horns rhythmic, chaotic, and all in a line.

Some danced, while others wept
in showers
or into their hands.
Just cupped whatever pieces of their flesh made sense
and let it wash over.

We all learned how to talk again
that day,
even if just for five minutes.
Whole conversations beginning with "I am"
ending with "feeling so good right now."
That was enough, really.
To let it sit there among the car horns and

the seagulls and for once in an immeasurable amount of time
   to expect
Nothing else.

Just those words.
Other words too, maybe, but nothing
heavier than the weight of a breath that finally
exhales.

What a strange day.
People got lost that day like other days, but this time
they danced off like an endless two-step
and let the spirit move them right out of the frame.

We readied ourselves to capture it all—
the misty, traceable feeling—
before it disappeared like the sun we knew would set
on this last day of warmth.

November had us crawling on our knees already—
and there is so much more to come.
But on this day, we duck from under the anchor and
we breathe in what we can.

It's not like it was just over a decade ago—we all know that.
There's no buoyancy here.
This lift in the air won't carry us to the end,
But some of us straddle it anyway
Roll our shoulders back, close our eyes, tilt our heads back
Mouth open

Over here, we gather by the ocean
My loves read me poems and leave packages

full of sweetness and scrawled words
on my lap.
We fill the air with our laughter and some tears
Almost forgetting that we work too much
and hurt too much
But holy fuck, this weather
Holy fuck, look at you
Beautiful & glistening, fully pulling air into your lungs,
down past your shoulder blades
fully resting on your back.
This sky is perfect. This ocean is perfect.
This crystalline moment is perfect.
It is a Saturday.

What We Owe and Are Owed

Kiese Laymon

Two days after an officer shot Ma'Khia Bryant in the back, and one day after an officer shot Andrew Brown in the back of the head, I asked my friend Ray Gunn if he was tired of talking to white folks about Black death. Gunn told me he didn't understand my question.

I repeated it.

Gunn asked if I was getting paid for these conversations I was having with white Americans about Black death. I told him sometimes. He asked me why I would ever talk to white folks about Black death if I wasn't getting paid.

"You know," I told him, "like on social media…"

Gunn shook his head.

"Or sometimes, you know, folks call you because they…"

Gunn sucked his teeth.

"I mean, I'm a teacher and you know, like…"

Gunn looked lightweight disgusted.

He reminded me that he was a teacher too. "But that," he said, "that's not Black teacher work. That's white family work."

Gunn told me he hadn't had an actual conversation with a white person in fourteen years, not out of protest but because there just weren't any white folks at his job, in his house, at his church, on his social media, or in his phone. "Now, if the check was right," he said, "I'd be a grinning, hustling-ass race whisperer. I'd be talking to everything white. Rice. Milk. Pillows."

I fell out laughing.

Gunn and I met in college in Jackson, Mississippi, twenty-eight years ago. I was a first-year student from Jackson and Gunn was a super-senior from Winona by way of Chicago. The first day I met Gunn, he was posted up in the quad, setting up a picnic for his partner, V.

Later that night, during our first conversation, he taught me how to make sure the ironed quilt you set out for your partner smelled like their second-favorite scent. "That means you gotta ask them what they favorite scents are," he told me. "If the quilt ain't ironed and smelling right, wash it and iron it again. Don't use starch though, unless that's her second-favorite smell. But you gotta ask."

Gunn knew he was talking about love.

I thought he was talking about "revision," a word our professors and high school teachers believed necessitated us reducing all of our Black rhetorical abundance into meager-ass absolutes. In my own sloppy work, on and off the page, I was beginning to understand "revision" as a dynamic practice of revisitation, premised on ethically reimagining the ingredients, scope, and primary audience of one's initial vision. Revision required witnessing and testifying. Witnessing and testifying required rigorous attempts at remembering and imagining. If revision was not God, revision was everything every God ever asked of believers.

In subsequent months, Gunn and I became boys, co-workers, cousins, forever family. When we weren't together, we talked about "we" and "us" far more than we talked about "I." We wrote En Vogue fan fiction. We memorized every word of *Menace II Society* and every syllable of *Ready to Die*. We invented words that should already have existed and new definitions for words as old as American exceptionalism.

We lived together in a tiny apartment on Capitol Street. We donated plasma for money right off of Fortification. We worked as porters on State Street. We stole white people's food when there was white people's food to be stolen. We borrowed massive cereal dispensers filled with Lucky Charms out of our college cafeteria because we were tired of Magic Stars. We jacked light bread off of bread trucks on the Reservoir. We dined, dashed, and left a tip at every Denny's in central Mississippi. We used Gunn's food stamps to get scallops and the good ramen to celebrate his little sister moving down to Mississippi.

We were poor. We were happy. We were not happy about being poor. But neither of us longed to be rich. We longed for healthy choices, second chances, and good love.

Then, after getting kicked out of our college for the theft of white folks' food—sike! I mean white folks' library books—I left Mississippi for Ohio, Indiana, and eventually New York.

When I returned to Mississippi twenty years later, even though my job was in a much more monied, neo-Confederate part of the state, I looked forward to living an hour from Gunn, who now worked as a teacher in a detention center for kids awaiting sentencing. I couldn't wait to regularly hear the wavy inflections in Gunn's voice when he did the opposite of humblebrag about his students and his own children's grades.

I wanted to act as if nothing had changed in our relationship since we first saw each other as young men. I wanted Gunn to forget the summer of 2010 when he asked if he could bring his daughter up to college where I taught in New York. We hadn't seen each other in six years. I agreed to take Gunn and his daughter on a tour of campus and then to the South Bronx, home of Gunn's favorite emcee.

I ended up lying about an emergency when they got to town because I didn't want Gunn to see that I'd gained more than 120 pounds since we'd last seen each other. I didn't want Gunn's daughter, my goddaughter, to look at me with disgust. I didn't want to be reminded of what I'd allowed my insides to become, nor the heart meat I'd become addicted to eating.

So I chose to harm all three of us. I lied, and I ran from my goddaughter and the one person on Earth I literally had no reason to run from.

Gunn told me he understood what I was saying because he'd lied and run from me, too. "We ain't young. We ain't even middle-aged," he said. "We just straight-up old and ain't no models of how to be straight-up old and Black and lonely. I lied to you so many times because I was ashamed. We here now."

I can't write about Ray Gunn without thinking about fairness and repair. In my laziness, I've conflated repair and restoration, just as I've lazily conflated pain with trauma, pleasure with desire, progress with liberation, honesty with truth, and fairness with equity. Restoration and repair are something we are worthy of in life and death, in relationships and solo, but they are not the same word.

Being a Black Mississippian means you will spend a lifetime repairing wounds created by the worst of white Mississippians in hopes of some kind of economic or moral renewal. This is not fair, nor is it fair that we are expected to make Black abundance out of that repair. This, however, is a part of our lineage.

The white family in America appears to have a lineage as well. The metastasized, excused unwellness in white families, monied and poor, is responsible for anti-Black terror happening in this nation's schools, prisons, hospitals, neighborhoods, and banks. This is the work of folks who despise revision nearly as much as they despise themselves. Abolish police, bullets, missiles, and prisons all we want (and some of us truly want!), and most white American families in the U.S. will do everything possible to make more. And in some ways, that's their business. Cleaning up the messes that seep from these families, we've been taught, is what Black folk in this nation do well.

But I don't want us to clean up the messes of white families. I want them to stop creating and pushing public policy that encourages us to die prematurely. I want them to pay my Grandmama what she is owed for a lifetime of literally, figuratively, and spiritually cleaning up their messes.

We have far too many messes of our own. At my worst, I have run away from our lineage of repair and renewal when I've harmed folks I loved. Every time we run away from an abusive mess, a negligent mess, a lethal mess we helped create, we leave something essential for someone targeted for premature death to clean up. That is humiliation.

That is not fair.

Family can help us repair. Family, chosen and by birth, can also significantly aid in helping those who eat our suffering effectively wipe us off the face of the earth. Repair what you helped break, my Grandmama taught me. Restore what responsibly loved you, I learned from Gunn. And revise, revise, revise with your family and friends. Collective freedom is impossible without interpersonal repair.

I'd hoped this piece could be an extended exploration of the paradoxical economic dimensions of Black friendship during the pandemic. I wanted this piece to open, fold, and crumple the tired ways we talk about revision in this nation. I wanted to write about Gunn's relationship to the state as a Black man who loves Black people, and a Black man who has found work in a detention center for mostly Black and Mexican young people.

But before I could write that, Gunn and I needed to talk with each other about what repair and renewal mean in our middle-age relationships with each other, with the dead, with the earth. We have to be as concerned with the question of what we're owed as we are with the question of what we owe us. I suspect, with rigorous, tender exploration, we will find that the answer to both of those questions is everything.

One morning in the spring of 1995, I woke up to this strange, nasally voice coming from the bathroom of the apartment Gunn and I shared. The voice was overenunciating the "or" sound in "elevatOR." The bathroom door was cracked and Gunn was in the mirror, not simply practicing talking "proper," but also practicing verbally and vocally becoming a Black man he imagined white folks might fairly compensate.

"Nigga," I remember saying to him through the door. "What are you doing?"

"Trying to get this money," he said.

During our most recent conversation, I asked Gunn if he remembers that day in 1995. After some uncomfortable silence, Gunn answered me. And we talked. And we listened. And we were honest about what we need for repair and what we might be incapable of sharing or accepting in this piece. Before hanging up, Gunn reiterated that Black people, especially poor Black people, need checks for the checks we've been shorted since we were brought here. Until those checks are issued, Gunn says again, he has nothing to say to white folks about the failings of white folks when he himself has failed so many Black folks.

I get it.

Near the end of my conversation with Gunn, he answered the goofy question, "Do you have hope in America?" with the only appropriate answer that should ever be given to that trite-ass question.

"I have faith in us."

When my editor at *Vox* asked me if I could write about "fairness" after the George Floyd verdict, I knew there was nothing new I could say to white Americans about their investments in Black suffering. It wasn't only that it had all been said, made, and written; it had all been said, made, and written by the greatest sayers, makers, and writers in history. So I started over, and I scrapped the traditional fetishizing portals of entry into anti-racism.

I decided I'd rather write to us and for us about the paradoxes of revision, restoration, and repair in our friendships. Instead of explaining something that has already been explained and making a spectacle of Black death, I decided to write something that makes me feel good about a man from Winona, Mississippi, who has loved me whole and halted my premature death.

Today, that is the most loving thing I can do to my insides and Gunn's. Today, that feels fair.

Get Well Slow

Josina Guess

You can't be sick now. It's the beginning of the school year. You just took a week away from work. You are vaccinated. But here you are, before sunset on a Saturday evening in August, shivering as you crawl into bed.

You have a fever all day Sunday. You text your boss to say you are having symptoms and will get tested Monday. You say you probably won't make the Wednesday meeting. You don't find it absurd that you are using the word *probably*. You sincerely believe you might sit up and be presentable for a nine o'clock video call—a challenge even on good days.

You still have a fever Monday morning when you schedule your appointment, then call a coworker to let her know you're "definitely not going to get much done today." Not much suggests you can still do, maybe, just a little of the work you let pile up from the previous week.

You notice the shower floor needs a good scrubbing after

a week of neglect, but you can't smell the bleach. You can't smell your favorite sandalwood soap when you wash the chemicals from your hands. Wiping down the shower was no herculean task, but you have to lie back down. You force yourself to get dressed to make it to your appointment at eleven. All you want to do is sleep. Still, you need confirmation of what you already know.

Your seventy-two-year-old father offers to drive, but you don't want him to risk infection by being in the car with you. You drive yourself. You park near an orange cone behind the clinic. The nurse comes out in a mask and a face shield; you roll down your window and remove your mask so she can scrape the untouched space below your eyes. The mask, the painful swab, the health care from a car, are routine at this point—you know the drill.

You remember early 2020 when this was all new, wondering if schools would close and if people would wear masks in public, wondering if you or anyone you know would get it. Ten minutes later, your nurse practitioner comes out to tell you it's positive, and your eyes get hot with tears. She tells you it's normal, that a lot of people with Covid experience a mixture of survivor guilt, fear, and something like PTSD; she herself went through it a year ago. She tells you to quarantine for ten days, drink lots of fluids, "control symptoms," call if things get worse. You cry as you drive home, shedding virus all over the steering wheel.

You don't think your symptoms will worsen. Ten days is a stretch, you think, and tell yourself you'll be better in five. You just learned the term "breakthrough infection" a month ago; this can't be serious. You text your boss a photo of your doctor's note, though you don't know why. You would never fake this, but the photo makes it real, justifies your continued absence.

Your phone pings. It's your boss: "I'm sorry. Rest, and I hope you get to feeling better. Let me know if there is anything I can do."

You can't tell people if there is anything they can do because that requires thinking, and right now your head is in a vice grip. You're sweaty and so unbelievably tired. You check email anyway.

You lie back down and text everyone you saw the previous week. You feel ashamed that you'd somehow let down your guard. For one glorious week, you sat in a graduate classroom, went out to eat, met new people, shook hands, hugged. You were a butterfly flitting about, drinking up the nectar of human connection beyond your bubble. You banish your husband to the couch and curl into the cocoon of your bedroom. Another classmate tests positive. Those first few days are a blur of short naps interrupted by updates, praying hands and hearts, healing vibes, and tears of relief when friends' and loved ones' tests come back negative.

On Wednesday, your father offers to make a breakfast sandwich. Eating meals at mealtime makes sense. You hear his footsteps before he calls your name through a mask and leaves the plate on the sideboard in the hall. The cheddar cheese is a layer of melted plastic, the egg a blob of silicone, the bacon provides a fatty crunch. The bagel is toasted, seedy Styrofoam. You tell him you can taste the love. You sleep through the staff meeting.

The vitamins your cousin ordered for you arrive in a smiling box. Bottles of Airborne tablets, zinc, D, C, aspirin, a thermometer, and a pulse oximeter clutter up your bedside table. Your friends and neighbors leave gifts of sourdough bread, chicken soup, borscht, a spray of fresh zinnias, and *The Parable of the Sower* on your porch. You eat bowl after bowl of spicy ramen, soba and miso soup with chunks of ginger and garlic, sliced jalapeños, mounds of kimchi. You feel a hint of sour on the side of your tongue, a whisper of hot in the back of your throat. Your father insists that you hold whole cloves in your mouth until you can taste their Christmas spice. You sweat and slurp and celebrate every faint glimmer of flavor and smell. You tell yourself you are getting better.

You sleep and sleep and sleep and sleep some more. You have hiked Copper Canyon carrying half your weight in water and gear. You have borne children. You've spent sleepless nights with ear-infected, vomiting infants. You have given around-the-clock antibiotics and B vitamins to your sick goat, waking to draw syringes before dawn. You have never felt this kind of tired.

Positive thinking can't wish this disease away, but you try anyway. You keep pushing yourself between naps. Your bed becomes a nest of books, papers, laptop, phone. You check on the garden, pick some tomatoes but go back in exhausted. Your body clearly can't handle any physical labor, but you try and trick it into thinking that brain work is okay. You keep taking calls, answering emails, reading, and following up with people from your sweaty, wrinkled sheets.

You reach the ten-day mark and declare yourself well. You return an empty soup pot to a neighbor with a thank-you note tucked inside.

On day eleven, a Friday, you miss the funeral for a local pastor and his daughter; the mother is dying in the ICU. This family survived war in Myanmar, arrived in the U.S. as refugees, only to die from a disease that you are surviving. At their graveside service, one of your friends urges everyone in attendance to get vaccinated to prevent more funerals.

That morning an infected and unvaccinated neighbor calls for advice. It is hard to understand the reasons for not getting vaccinated, but you want everyone, even the people you don't understand, to make it through this.

By eleven your power goes out, the internet is down, and you can't get through the day. The outage forces you to do what you should have done on day one: stop. The weekend passes in a fog. The pastor's wife dies on Sunday.

That third week is the hardest because you finally surrender to the focused work of healing just when everyone is ready for you to be better. You charge your phone and laptop in another room; calls and emails go unanswered. The meals stop coming, and your father decides it's time to go back home. Your husband and children miss you cracking jokes around the dinner table and helping find lost shoes. Every time you test the waters of normalcy, you are facedown on your pillow. You feel the hag riding you.

In the blur of illness and solitude, you watch documentaries and listen to podcasts about ghosts and reincarnation. You read about hauntings and young children's memories of previous lives and deaths. What will the babies of the early 2020s remember? Will they find themselves gasping for breath? What ghosts is this pandemic making?

The vaccine protected your lungs and kept you out of the hospital, kept you among the living. Nevertheless, your fight with the virus has made the veil so thin, your spirit so thankful to still inhabit your body.

Hurricane Ida hits at the end of August, and you text your friend in New Orleans to see how her home weathered another storm. She and her family were among the first confirmed cases of Covid-19. Eighteen months later, she still has symptoms—nerve pain, fatigue, brain fog—and her son's farts smell like sweeTARTS to her. She confirms that what you are feeling is real.

In early September, one month after testing positive, you take a family vacation to Edisto, a South Carolina sea island. You let the ocean hold you, let the sun and wind kiss you dry. You ask your children to bury you up to your neck in the sand. You are born again.

By October, coffee still tastes bitter, but you like it again. Friends ask if you are all the way better and you say, "Yes, I think." The exhaustion comes in waves. You question every sniffle, pain, and forgotten word. You get winded talking on the phone while walking. You are teaching yourself to do one thing at a time.

You used to say *get well soon, speedy recovery, hope you are back on your feet in no time.* But now you will say only, *rest.* Rest. Take the time you need to rest. Let the grass grow tall. Let the laundry and dishes pile up. Let the emails and texts and phone calls go unanswered. Let the weeds overtake your flower beds. Let the tomatoes rot on the vine, the okra turn to wood, and the milk go sour. Let the mold grow on your shower floor. Let the children go feral, their clothes wrinkled and unwashed.

Call for help. Accept help. But if the asking feels like work, requires too much thinking and directing and planning, just let it go.

Just let go. Get well slow. Claim rest as holy work.

Whosoever Will, Come On In

Imani e Wilson

"You know, I used to go to church…but Black people
know God personally. Any wino you meet
know God…right? Or Jesus, at least."

—Richard Pryor, *Wattstax* (1973)

I miss church in all of its incarnations, and they are myriad.
No matter what form it takes, song/dance is at the center. The
thinned-out coda of a party that lasts until sunrise, peopled
by the most serious dancers. Borough Day in Point Fortin in
the South of Trinidad. When the block party DJ dials down
the volume on "Sir Duke," "Lovely Day," or "I Wanna Thank
You" so that we can show and prove. We don't need no music.
We are a musical infinity and then some. Church is a way of
knowing and a mode of being. It is a stone groove. In Cory
Henry and TaRon Lockett's virtually reconstituted Revival—
live-streaming "services" on Sunday afternoons throughout
the pandemic—I recall that Church, writ large, is also a collapsed time, an invisible space.

At the last church service I attended before the pandemic,
the preacher was in Exodus 12, the text that tells of the plagues
visited upon Egypt in the context of our snowballing fear of

a virus that was making its way across the globe, snatching lives as it went. The children of Israel, still enslaved, were instructed to put the blood of a lamb on the frames of their doors as a signal to the death angel to pass over. That was on March 9, 2020, and from here, I see that was also the anniversary of B.I.G.'s passing. Absent choir rehearsal and Sunday worship, church anniversaries, shut-ins, and night service, the church has hovered in what I call the Between Time. I dream of being in the sanctuary.

28 August 2020

Yesterday a tornado tore through this street taking the power with it. Last night in the pitch black quiet I sank into deep sleep and dreamt of church. I was in a pew on the balcony, with Cheryl seated on my right-hand side. A mirror image of what would have been were things set right. The Cathedral felt different, the altar more distant. Why aren't we in the choir loft? And who is that in the tenor section? Why are we here? When did we come back? "I looked at my hands," like the song lyrics say, and noted that we were without masks but I didn't say anything. Maybe I had dreamt the plague or I had lived through it and now suddenly found myself dropped back into a clean, safe reality. After service, I exited the sanctuary, walked down a hallway, and entered an empty classroom where I sat down and cried.

It must be the music because everything else in the service can come, go, or change. What sounds churchy can be mapped to geography and denomination, the trombones of the United House of Prayer in one quarter, slack key guitar in another, quartet singing with four on the floor and a snare shuffle yonder. I came up here in New York, with the music of Brooklyn Pentecostals. "Old New York groove!" is how Hezekiah Walker describes the drive on a recording.

The organists defined the sound: Professor Alfred White, Professor Butch Heyward, Reverend Timothy Wright, Bishop Nathaniel Townsley, Bishop Jeffrey White. And the generations that followed behind them: James "Jazzy" Hall, Stanley Brown, Melvin Crispell, Jules Bartholomew, Roger Jean, Travis Sayles, Glenn Gibson, Stephen Ballard, and Cory Henry. The organ is indispensable and it is enough. To my ear, the B-3 is church.

While their keyboards have a common layout, the Hammond B-3 is not a piano; the Fender Rhodes is another thing again, and auxiliary keys require a different kind of expertise. Cory Henry is a master of all of them. The Hammond offers an orchestra of timbre, requires all four limbs and a mind that will organize them into a seamless sound. Cory Henry, whose storied career on the B-3 began at age two, pioneered the organ and drum project that he calls The Revival with a live recording in East New York on a steamy Saturday night in September 2014. Today, The Revival consists of Henry and TaRon Lockett, the drummer from his band The Funk Apostles. Using a complex rig of cameras, phones, computers, and mics to capture and broadcast their stylings, they make magic on Twitch, YouTube, Facebook, and Instagram.

Each Sunday, he and TaRon Lockett use the Hammond B-3 organ and the drum kit to fashion a building not made by hands. Henry explains: "Revival music is just music that makes us feel good." It fits in nicely with other church-speak: "She thought it not robbery," "on tonight," "man(d) of God," and "I can't get no help in here." In a studio on occasion, but most often at home, Henry and Lockett offer an hour, or two, of power. I watch the Quarantine Sessions of The Revival on Twitch, which has superior audio. There the comments scroll past at a clip and allow listeners to replicate the responses they would offer were they hearing the music live and in person. The churched among us say "amen." We name the hymns and choir repertoire, identifying the recording artist whose version is the accepted standard, point out the doxology that opens the set. Cory Henry's fans tune in from Japan, Brazil, South Africa, France, Italy, Scotland, and Australia, and request that he play originals or Chick Corea's "Spain." They ask him to switch to the Fender Rhodes.

We extend our antennae, seeking a signal. Scanning for the sets we had hoped to hear, shows we planned to experience, services we expected to sing. We attempt to connect. In addition to The Revival, I pick up D-Nice and Clark Kent's Sunday SCQool set, DJ Reborn's Sign Language, watch Ronald K. Brown's *Evidence*, and listen to Kiese Laymon in conversation with his aunt, Rev. Carolyn Coleman. I bear witness as we celebrate the ascent of DMX, crown him with the "Ruff Ryders Anthem" rendered ethereal by the pitch-perfect arrangements of Jason White sung by The Samples. All of it is sacred ground. Church all around.

It is no secret: Cory Henry is here on a sound mission, sent to move minds, hearts, and bodies. He plays and sings with authority, has the kind of gift that comes with explicit permission to handle each song like it is his very last time. Not for the musical fireworks, but for some ear, some last nerve, some soul that needs a dose of musical medicine. His is a life-saving sound. Before the pandemic, on the best of Sundays, after worship was underway at my home church, the Greater Allen Cathedral in Jamaica, Queens, I'd see Cory Henry slide through the side door, dap up the brother from the security ministry and appear at the edge of the altar, motorcycle helmet in hand. Singing in the choir was a source of joy, but singing on a Sunday when Cory Henry was playing? Man…listen.

I remember revival proper. It was not an event but a process measured in weeks. When I was a child growing up in Queens, I attended revivals at Allen, but Bethel held their revival in Roy Wilkins Park. In those days, even if it was a weeknight service conducted out of doors, I wore a dress and pantyhose. A mantilla, the lace bobby-pinned to my hair, completed my uniform—a costume that communicated, "I know the rules. I belong here."

More than anything I witnessed after taking my seat in the service, I remember the sound as I approached. Before you could get under the tent, you experienced the revival as an undeniable rhythm and drive, bounce and pop. The bass could rattle your rib cage, and you found your footfall matching the two and four of the bass drum. To my eyes, everything visible was in thrall to that sound. The leaves and branches swaying slightly against the backdrop of the twilight sky did so in time. The streetlights powered up on the one. The music beckoned, offering invite and embrace. It was not for me or anybody else who had been at church on Sunday. Revival is shelter without walls, a reconfigured welcome. Whosoever will, come on in the room.

The truest me shows up in the space, with those people, our rites, each suspended chord, every turnaround of a refrain that won't turn us aloose. There, my essence is called forth into the open. She steps forward in sync with a tambourine whose perfect timing evinces all of eternity. It is not that this self is ever absent, but rather that she is fully welcome there. Church has offered me the landing place that a family barbecue offers the youngest child in attendance. The new addition is held and admired, loved out loud, and made accountable for her gifts. "Determine and decide who you are up inside here, where you belong, where we love and claim you...because, girl, what lies beyond the gate doesn't bear description." For the elders, Little One is a reminder of why they've pressed on. They encourage her to dance with their loved ones, in the presence of a great cloud of witnesses. "Get it! Aww, shucks…come on now."

I grasped that music was the thing that held me together, a tight embrace. Whether vinyl spun in a lounge, banging on a car stereo or played and sung live in church, sound and movement made me whole, where glue stick, rubber cement, gum, and bakery box twine could not. Music is my extreme measure, all over me and keeping me alive. When I heard the sure groove of a praise song, the hymns played softly to give you a chance to pull yourself together after prayer, I recognized the sound waves calmed my anxiety and steadied my breath. The love and joy conveyed in that space stood proxy for what I did not and could not feel. Like Ash and Chelsey Barnes sing, *When in doubt and despair, anytime, anywhere.* Music is grace.

> *I thank Him for the storms He brought me through.*
> *For if I'd never had a problem,*
> *I wouldn't know God could solve them…*

As I struggle to see a way forward or a reason to keep trying to see a way, I am playing The Revival at full volume. This particularly bright May afternoon, Cory Henry is playing "Through It All" in a total mind meld with TaRon Lockett. I am simultaneously hearing the original recording for the first time, complete with needle drop and vinyl crackle. I'm sitting at Aunt Claudine's piano, playing along with the cassette on my Walkman. It is the mid-1980s and Andraé Crouch and The Disciples are playing through a thick veneer of AM radio static on WWRL, because New York City is too heathen to have a proper gospel station. It is 2018 and I am in silent tears driving a New England highway listening to "Through It All" on CD.

At the same time, I am in St. Mark Holy Church at 1980 Fulton Street, in Bed-Stuy, where Bishop Nathaniel Townsley Jr. is the senior pastor. I am seated on the center aisle on Palm Sunday, April 14, 2019. Bishop Townsley is leading service from the organ; and as it often does at St. Mark, a music church, song is driving the service. An audio recording from that day tells me that a mighty, rushing wind swept through that room and left me weeping, heaving sobs of relief, grateful for a recently averted disaster. I don't recall any of that, but I do remember Bishop playing and singing Andráe Crouch's "Take Me Back" as communion was passed.

A year later, on Palm Sunday 2020, Bishop Nathaniel Townsley Jr. left here for glory. That morning, locked down and at loose ends, missing church, I had watched every video I could find of Bishop. In a three minute, thirty-five second clip, Bishop Townsley plays the B-3 and key bass, Junie is on the kit and Jonathan Dubose is on guitar when all of their heads turn to acknowledge a presence beyond the frame. Over a head-nodding vamp, Bishop leads while Dubose and unseen vocalists harmonize the refrain *I can do anything* when whoever is recording pans right and we see the figure that has Bishop's attention. It is a young Cory Henry that Bishop is calling forward to take over the key bass he is playing with his left hand.

Part of what makes church is proximity. There are people behind and in front of me, and my dress sleeve might brush the arm of the stranger on my right. I can smell the pink lotion I used to set my bangs and wonder if they can too. We are close-close, so when I sing, the sound waves coming from my mouth meet the ones sung by the folk sitting on my row. I can reach out and touch sound; it is tangible and textured. It changes the space, sets the atmosphere. Under its sway, I discover that I too am mutable, liable to be made over, overcome, to weep, take off running, brace my dancing self on a wall with my fingertips. It is not unusual for me to shut my eyes, open my arms wing-wide, and fall out under the weight of a glory cloud. My body knifing through the air backward, approaching a solid floor as swiftly as I might dive into the sea. The B-3 is a sure vehicle from one dimension to another.

It was there all the time. On records, I'd heard it lingering behind the piano, the power of which was beginning to unfold beneath my tentative fingers in piano lessons with Ms. Anne S. Williams in Saturday morning lessons. I was raised up right, which meant that there was music waiting on me when I got here. The organ was another order of being, animated by electricity, a low-grade whir announcing its potential as soon as it was powered up, the blades of the Leslie cabinet gathering the air in a room, molding and shaping it before sending it back out into space. In our basement with headphones, a mixer, a pair of Technics S-arms, and reel-to-reel tape, my father built me a world of sound. There the Hammond was ubiquitous though still invisible, like paint on the walls.

Earl "Wya" Lindo's percussive comping bubbled beneath The Wailers' "Hallelujah Time." That warning siren at the top of "Rock Steady" is Donny Hathaway bringing sunspot heat to Aretha's indelible groove. That is James Brown self playing trills on "Make It Funky." In my mind's eye, I saw hands. I could intuit that much by hearing; the organ wasn't played with a bow like Noel Pointer's violin or breath like Bobbi Humphrey's flute. I did not imagine the permutations of the drawbars that offered a full orchestra of choices, nor the footboard that magnified the keyboard to allow a left foot to dance the bassline. The Hammond B-3 and the Leslie also made possible the confounding magic of Billy Preston, Danny Hawkins, and Elbernita "Twinkie" Clark.

> "It happens that the beginnings of creation
> are hard to tell apart from mere destruction."
> —*Two Thousand Seasons*, Ayi Kwei Armah

Let the death dealer speak of endings. It is our way to begin again, make ourselves deeply present to possibility. The doors of the church are yet closed. In empty sanctuaries or on soundstages, preachers talk directly to cameras in a vacuum emptied of hearers. This Sunday, The Revival, live on Twitch, is the last remnant of church that I can identify. This music that my soul requires appears in installments like musical manna, wilderness quail. Perched on my kitchen table, the flat screen that the Jetsons promised me comes alive with songs that mark the way back to life.

Deliberate as architecture and effortless like a summertime growth spurt, this is love. Lightning strobes and makes our surroundings truly visible, breaking the moving image down to a series of stills, each frame a perfectly focused snapshot. The bass coalesces in thunderheads and the floor tom directs a complex footwork sequence.

now. *Pick 'em up*

&

there! *Lay 'em down.*

That step gathers speed and finally lifts off into a spin. It floats up from the silence then fades to a distant crackle.

"This is my happy song. I sing it around the house and it normally works. It is better than medicine," Cory Henry shares over the changes of "Naa Naa Naa."

213

Music feels like fire shut up in my bones, he sings, and I two-step in my kitchen to this chant that flips on a light switch deep on the inside. It gives way to "God Be With You," an old song that we haven't sung in recent years as often as I think we should. *Treat the people you meet with love, 'cuz love is all we have and love is all we need.*

Finally we receive the benediction, the congregation in Scotland and Rio de Janeiro, South Africa, and Tokyo, in his hometown of Brooklyn and adopted city, Los Angeles. "Live in love, live in peace, grow in freedom." Chief Apostle Cory Henry ends the virtual broadcast as he would a show in person. All hearts and minds are clear.

As the world reconstitutes in person, I wonder how many Sundays of Quarantine Sessions remain. Cory Henry and TaRon Lockett play till their souls get happy and sometimes until they laugh themselves silly. Singing "Uncloudy Day" at the request of his Aunt Van, Cory's eyes well up and overflow but the tears do not interfere with his tone. "My mother used to sing this." His tears and the mention of his late mother call to the well of tears in me. As I cry, the sound leaves me steadied, strengthened. I feel my help.

I dread returning to St. Mark for worship and not seeing my Bishop on the organ. I have not made peace with the fact that he won't give me one more lesson, not in person. The Cathedral will be open next Sunday and, within twenty minutes of receiving word via email, all the seats are taken. Perhaps for another week, I can stave off being bowled over by the crash of a wave of emotion that awaits me in the sanctuary. Also waiting for me at church, beyond the crash, the sea rushes back out to the deep and in the hush, in the reunion and the remaking, I believe I will find peace. Soon come.

When New Year's Day lands on a Sunday, we greet the midnight hour with a shout, with prayers, hugs, and tears. We celebrate and cross over knowing we have to return before first light for 6:30 service. Watch night is a service where music and dance are given primacy of place and the band is still playing pure fire when the preacher says "...be dismissed from this place but never from God's presence." As Sister Evelyn and I button our coats, when I hug Mother Connie, I say, "Traveling mercies." "Okay, now. Get home safe," each replies. I gather encore benedictions on my way out into the frigid blast.

There is no need to say good-bye. Whether here or on the other side, I will see you in the morning.

Another Quarantine Blues

Kamilah Aisha Moon

I sit in the backyard
bathed in birdsong
& the funky ballads
of a rural Black man
named Bill who strummed
& belted his blues
into a golden legacy
he just left behind,
manna for hearts
that have yet to give out.

A lovely day,
the breeze caresses
what hasn't been
caressed for so long
as I miss
who moves me—
something massive
yet imperceptible
sways among
the green frenzy
unfurling high
above my head.

It is April. A spiked virus
rampages yet I feel like
a child encountering
lavender for the first time,
riveted by the saffron beaks
of robins, the crimson blur
of cardinals, the regal
swoop of blue jays, majestic
without the need to rule.

Water quenches like never before.

In my deepest recesses,
I recall sapling life
in a divine grove—
not yet a woman
crumbling into a heap
of sad diagnoses
& heavy sobs.
A travesty is to be
so divorced
from thriving
I didn't know
that wisteria grows
mere feet in soft grass
from where I dream
on nights silvered
by grace.

Another friend coughs
in the ghosted city,
becomes a memory.

Kamilah Aisha Moon

If spared, I swear
to savor sacred time
on my small patch
of borrowed earth,
letting the trees offer
what they always have
as natural, priceless
ventilators—
silent, holy company!
Sweet shade from
all things glaring.

About the Contributors

SAMAA ABDURRAQIB's writing can be found in *Bad Girls and Transgressive Women in Popular Television, Fiction, and Film*; *Enough! Poems of Resistance and Protest*; and the online platform *The Body Is Not an Apology*. She published her first poetry chapbook, *Each Day Is Like an Anchor*, in 2020. Samaa lives in the unceded territory of the Wabanaki people and spends much of her free time recreating in the outdoors, enjoying the waterways, mountains, birds, and woods.

ROSALIND BENTLEY is the interim director of the narrative nonfiction MFA program in the Grady College of Journalism and Mass Communication at the University of Georgia. She is also deputy editor at the Southern Foodways Alliance's journal, *Gravy*, and editor at large for the *Oxford American*. She is a Pulitzer Prize finalist and two-time James Beard Award finalist.

EMILY BERNARD is the author of *Black Is the Body*, winner of the Los Angeles Times–Christopher Isherwood Prize for Auto-biographical Prose. She is a 2020 Andrew Carnegie Fellow and the Julian Lindsay Green and Gold Professor of English at the University of Vermont.

DESTINY O. BIRDSONG is the author of the poetry collection *Negotiations*, which was published by Tin House Books in 2020 and longlisted for the 2021 PEN/Voelcker Award, and the triptych novel *Nobody's Magic*, which was published by Grand Central in 2022.

PEARL CLEAGE is currently Distinguished Artist in Residence at the Alliance Theatre in Atlanta. Her most recent play, *Angry, Raucous, and Shamelessly Gorgeous*, premiered at the Alliance in 2019. She was commissioned in 2021 by the Ford's Theatre Legacy Commissions to complete a new history play, *Something Moving: A Meditation on Maynard*.

DANIEL B. COLEMAN is a Black trans artist-scholar invested in pluriversal possibilities for knowledge production and practice. He is an assistant professor of Black feminist thought, sexuality, and queer studies at Georgia State University. You can read more about his work at danielbcoleman.com.

LOLIS ERIC ELIE is a New Orleans-born, Los Angeles based television writer and essayist. His essay "America's Greatest Hits" was included in the 2010 edition of *Best African American Essays*. His books include *Smokestack Lightning* and *Treme: Stories and Recipes from the Heart of New Orleans*. His television credits include *Treme* and *The Man in the High Castle*.

AUNJANUE ELLIS-TAYLOR is a two-time Emmy nominee, as well as a Golden Globe, Critics Choice, BAFTA, and Oscar nominee. Her essays appear in *TIME* and *EBONY*, and on CNN. She is the coauthor, with her sister, of the forthcoming graphic novel *Neshoba* from Amistad/HarperCollins. She lives proudly somewhere in backwoods Wi-Fi Never Works, Mississippi.

B. BRIAN FOSTER is a Mississippi writer currently working as associate professor of sociology at the University of Virginia. His book *I Don't Like the Blues: Race, Place, and the Backbeat of Black Life* tells the story of blues development and Black community life in the Mississippi Delta town of Clarksdale.

LATRIA GRAHAM is a writer living in South Carolina. Her work often sits at the intersection of southern culture, gender norms, class, and environmental racism and is featured in the *Atlantic*, the *Guardian*, the *New York Times*, *Garden & Gun*, and the *Oxford American*. You can find more of her work at latriagraham.com.

JOSINA GUESS is a writer, mother, farmer, and editor based near Athens, Georgia. Her work appears in *Ecotone*, *Fourth Genre*, *About Place Journal*, and *Sojourners*. She is a senior writer for the *Bitter Southerner* and is enrolled in the narrative nonfiction MFA program at the University of Georgia.

ALEXIS PAULINE GUMBS is a queer Black feminist love evangelist and an aspirational cousin to all life. Alexis is also the author of several books, most recently *Undrowned: Black Feminist Lessons from Marine Mammals* and *Dub: Finding Ceremony*. She was a 2020–2021 National Humanities Center Fellow and is a current National Endowment for the Arts Creative Writing Fellow. Her biography *The Eternal Life of Audre Lorde* is forthcoming. She is cofounder of Mobile Homecoming Trust in Durham, North Carolina.

IDA HARRIS is an essayist and journalist writing at the intersection of Blackness and womanhood. Her work is featured in *Boston Review*, *ELLE*, *ESSENCE*, *YES! Magazine*, *USA TODAY*, and more. As a New York native, she represents South Jamaica, Queens—and considers the South home. She is currently an MFA candidate at the University of Mississippi and managing editor for *MadameNoire*.

HONORÉE FANONNE JEFFERS is the author of five books of poetry, including *The Gospel of Barbecue* and *The Age of Phillis*, and one novel, *The Love Songs of W.E.B. Du Bois*. A native southerner, Jeffers now lives on the prairie and teaches creative writing at the University of Oklahoma.

New York Times best-selling writer and 2021 Guggenheim Fellow **TAYARI JONES** is the author of four novels. Jones is a graduate of Spelman College, University of Iowa, and Arizona State University.

She is an Andrew D. White Professor-at-Large at Cornell University and the Charles Howard Candler Professor of Creative Writing at Emory University.

KIESE LAYMON is a Black southern writer from Jackson, Mississippi. He is the author of the novel *Long Division*, the essay collection *How to Slowly Kill Yourself and Others in America*, and the *New York Times* best-selling *Heavy: An American Memoir*.

KAREN GOOD MARABLE is an Atlanta-based writer whose byline has been featured in books and magazines including the *New Yorker*, the *Bitter Southerner*, and *ESSENCE*. She is particularly proud of the essay in this anthology. In late July 2020, while originally penning "Joyride" for the *Oxford American*, her family contracted Covid. Through phlegm, short breath, no taste, and worry, still she wrote—and is grateful to tell the tale.

E. ETHELBERT MILLER is a literary activist and author of two memoirs and several poetry collections. He hosts *On the Margin with E. Ethelbert Miller* (WPFW) and hosts and produces *The Scholars* (UDC-TV), which received a 2020 Telly Award. Miller's latest book is *When Your Wife Has Tommy John Surgery and Other Baseball Stories*, published by City Point Press.

KAMILAH AISHA MOON was the author of *Starshine & Clay* and *She Has a Name*, a finalist for the Lambda Literary Award for Lesbian Poetry and the Audre Lorde Award from the Publishing Triangle. Her other honors included a Pushcart Prize and fellowships from Cave Canem, the Fine Arts Work Center, MacDowell, the Prague Summer Writing Institute, and the Vermont Studio Center. She taught poetry at Rikers Island and Medgar Evers College, CUNY, in New York City. She then taught at Agnes Scott College in Atlanta, Georgia, where she lived until her passing on September 24, 2021.

OPAL MOORE is the author of *Lot's Daughters* and text collaborator for *Children of Middle Passage*, a perpetual performance artwork with artist Arturo Lindsay. She lives and writes in Atlanta, Georgia.

JASMIN PITTMAN MORRELL is a writer featured in *Meeting at the Table: African-American Women Write on Race, Culture, and Community*; the *Porch*; and the *Bitter Southerner*. She teaches creative nonfiction at Lenoir-Rhyne University, and alongside her family, loves calling the mountains of western North Carolina home.

REYNA NORIEGA, whose artwork is featured on the cover, is an Afro-Caribbean Latina visual artist and author. She was born, raised, and now works in Miami, Florida. Having seen the power of self-reflection, she illustrates our journeys as we rise to our most authentic selves. She aims to fill the world with vibrant, joyful depictions of marginalized people, centering women of color. Her work has graced magazine covers including *Science* and the *New Yorker*, and thousands of people collect and showcase her art in their homes.

IMANI PERRY is the Hughes-Rogers Professor of African American Studies at Princeton University. She is the author, most recently, of *South to America: A Journey Below the Mason-Dixon to Understand the Soul of a Nation* and *Looking for Lorraine: The Radiant and Radical Life of Lorraine Hansberry*, winner of the 2019 Bograd Weld Award for Biography from PEN America. She is also the author of *Breathe: A Letter to My Sons*, *Vexy Thing: On Gender and Liberation*, and *May We Forever Stand: A History of the Black National Anthem*.

DEESHA PHILYAW's debut story collection, *The Secret Lives of Church Ladies*, won the 2021 PEN/Faulkner Award for Fiction, the 2020/2021 Story Prize, and the 2020 Los Angeles Times Book Prize: The Art Seidenbaum Award for First Fiction. It was a finalist for the National Book Award for Fiction.

KHADIJAH QUEEN, PhD, is the author of six books, most recently *Anodyne*, published by Tin House Books in 2020, and *I'm So Fine: A List of Famous Men & What I Had On*, published by YesYes Books in 2017. She is an associate professor of creative writing at Virginia Tech.

JASON REYNOLDS is an award-winning and *New York Times* best-selling author of many books, including *Stamped: Racism, Antiracism, and You*, a collaboration with Ibram X. Kendi; *Long Way Down*; *Look Both Ways*; and the Track series.

SHARAN STRANGE teaches writing at Spelman College. Her recent work appears in *The Art Section: An Online Journal of Art and Cultural Commentary* and *Aunt Chloe: A Journal of Artful Candor*, and the anthologies *Black Imagination* and *Furious Flower: Seeding the Future of African American Poetry*. Her writings have also been included in gallery and museum exhibitions in New York, Boston, Atlanta, Oakland, and Seattle, and her collaborations with composers have been performed by American Modern Ensemble, The Dream Unfinished Orchestra, and International Contemporary Ensemble, among others.

ALICE WALKER is the acclaimed author of novels, stories, essays, and poetry. In 1983, she became the first African American woman to win a Pulitzer Prize for fiction for her novel *The Color Purple*, which also won the National Book Award. Among her other books are *The Temple of My Familiar*, *Meridian*, *Possessing the Secret of Joy*, and *Gathering Blossoms Under Fire*, edited by Valerie Boyd.

KAMILLE D. WHITTAKER is a California-born, Jamaica-nurtured journalist, editor, and instructor living and mothering in the South.

IMANI e WILSON is a writer, arts educator, and choir member. A born-and-raised New Yorker of Caribbean parentage, Wilson is an independent scholar whose work centers Black song/dance, shared memory, and soul thought. She is writing a collection of essays titled *Deep: What We Sing Down Here Below*.

L. LAMAR WILSON's documentary poetics animate *Sacrilegion*, published by Carolina Wren Press in 2013, and *The Changing Same*, a 2019 collaboration with Rada Film Group for POV Shorts, which streams at American Documentary and airs on PBS. He teaches creative writing, African American poetics, and film studies at Florida State University.

SHAY YOUNGBLOOD is a writer, educator, and interdisciplinary artist. She is the author of novels, including *Black Girl in Paris*, children's books, essays, and plays. Her short stories have been performed at Symphony Space and recorded for NPR's *Selected Shorts*. Youngblood received an MFA from Brown University. She teaches in the graduate creative writing program at the City College of New York, and is a board member of Yaddo artist retreat.

Acknowledgments

Samaa Abdurraqib, "November 7, 2020" ©2022 by Samaa Abdurraqib.

Rosalind Bentley, "Iron and Brass" ©2022 by Rosalind Bentley.

Emily Bernard, "The Purpose of a House" from the *New Yorker*, June 25, 2020. ©2020 by Emily Bernard. Reprinted by permission of the author.

Destiny O. Birdsong, "Build Back a Body" from *Ecotone* 16.1 ©2020 by Destiny O. Birdsong. Reprinted by permission of the author.

Valerie Boyd, "Profit and Loss" ©2022 by Valerie Boyd.

Jericho Brown, "Crossing" from *The Tradition*. Copyright ©2019 by Jericho Brown. Reprinted with the permission of The Permissions Company, LLC on behalf of Copper Canyon Press, coppercanyonpress.org.

Pearl Cleage, "Just Like Now" ©2022 by Pearl Cleage.

Daniel B. Coleman, "Pandemics and Portals: Listening That Breaks Us Open" ©2022 by Daniel B. Coleman.

Lolis Eric Elie, "A Survivor Looks Back" ©2022 by Lolis Eric Elie.

Aunjanue Ellis-Taylor, "The Women Who Clean" ©2022 by Aunjanue Ellis-Taylor.

ABOUT THE TYPE

This book is set in Freight, a versatile and enduring typeface designed in 2005 by Joshua Darden, one of the first known Black typeface designers. Darden began designing type at age sixteen, and in 2004, established Darden Studio, a Brooklyn-based foundry. He describes Freight Text and Sans—just two of Freight's 120 fonts—as an "elusive balance of warmth, energy, and pragmatism." This flexibility allowed for the exclusive use of Freight throughout *Bigger Than Bravery*.

TEXT   FREIGHT TEXT PRO BOOK   10.8 / 14.8
DISPLAY   FREIGHT BIG PRO BOLD   22

Lookout is more than a name—it's our publishing philosophy. Housed in the University of North Carolina Wilmington's nationally ranked creative writing department, Lookout Books brings attention to works by emerging and historically underrepresented writers, as well as overlooked gems by established authors, and offers students apprenticeships in the art and craft of publishing.

Thanks to Lookout faculty KaToya Ellis Fleming and Emily Louise Smith, and to students Amanda Ake, Marissa Castrigno, Cheyenne Faircloth, Daniel Grear, Zoe Howard, Lauran Jones, Lindsay Lake, Olivia Loorz, Vasilios Moschouris, Katherine O'Hara, Sarah Mina Osman, Luca Rhatigan, Gabi Stephens, Laura Traister, Felicia Rosemary Urso, Ryleigh Wann, and Morissa M. Young for their dedication to this project. With additional gratitude to Publishing Laboratory Assistant Director Michael Ramos and Administrative Associate Siobahn Daugherty.